Other titles by James N. Loehlin:

Henry V (Shakespeare in Performance, Manchester University Press)
Romeo and Juliet (Shakespeare in Production, Cambridge University Press)
Chekhov: The Cherry Orchard (Plays in Production, Cambridge University Press)
Henry IV: Parts I and II (The Shakespeare Handbooks, Palgrave Macmillan)
The Cambridge Introduction to Chekhov

THE SHAKESPEARE HANDBOOKS

Series Editors: Paul Edmondson and Kevin Ewert
(Founding Series Editor: John Russell Brown)

PUBLISHED

David Carnegie	*Julius Caesar*
Paul Edmondson	*Twelfth Night*
Bridget Escolme	*Antony and Cleopatra*
Kevin Ewert	*Henry V*
Alison Findlay	*Much Ado About Nothing*
Trevor R. Griffiths	*The Tempest*
Stuart Hampton-Reeves	*Measure for Measure*
Stuart Hampton-Reeves	*Othello*
Margaret Jane Kidnie	*The Taming of the Shrew*
Ros King	*The Winter's Tale*
James N. Loehlin	*Henry IV: Parts I and II*
Jeremy Lopez	*Richard II*
Christopher McCullough	*The Merchant of Venice*
Paul Prescott	*Richard III*
Edward L. Rocklin	*Romeo and Juliet*
John Russell Brown	*Hamlet*
John Russell Brown	*King Lear*
John Russell Brown	*Macbeth*
Lesley Wade Soule	*As You Like It*
Martin White	*A Midsummer Night's Dream*

SHAKESPEARE'S CONTEMPORARIES

Marshall Botvinick	*Jonson: Volpone*
David Carnegie	*Webster: The Duchess of Malfi*
James N. Loehlin	*Marlowe: Doctor Faustus*
Jay O'Berski	*Middleton and Rowley: The Changeling*
Stephen Purcell	*Webster: The White Devil*
Martin White	*Ford: 'Tis Pity She's a Whore*

Other titles are currently in preparation.

The Shakespeare Handbooks
Shakespeare's Contemporaries

Christopher Marlowe
Doctor Faustus

James N. Loehlin

First published 2016 by
PALGRAVE

Palgrave in the UK is an imprint of Macmillan Publishers Limited,
registered in England, company number 785998, of 4 Crinan Street,
London, N1 9XW.

Palgrave Macmillan in the US is a division of St Martin's Press LLC,
175 Fifth Avenue, New York, NY 10010.

Palgrave is a global imprint of the above companies and is represented
throughout the world.

Palgrave® and Macmillan® are registered trademarks in the United States,
the United Kingdom, Europe and other countries.

ISBN 978–1–137–42634–5 hardback
ISBN 978–1–137–42633–8 paperback

This book is printed on paper suitable for recycling and made from fully
managed and sustained forest sources. Logging, pulping and manufacturing
processes are expected to conform to the environmental regulations of the
country of origin.

A catalogue record for this book is available from the British Library.

Library of Congress Cataloging-in-Publication Data
Loehlin, James N.
   Marlowe : Doctor Faustus / James N. Loehlin.
     pages cm. – (Shakespeare handbooks)
   Summary: "This introductory guide to one of Marlowe's most widely-studied plays
offers a scene-by-scene theatrically aware commentary, a brief history of the text
and first performances, case studies of key performances and productions, a survey
of screen adaptations, and a wide sampling of critical opinion and further reading"–
Provided by publisher.
     ISBN 978–1–137–42633–8 (paperback) — ISBN 978–1–137–42634–5 (hardback)
     1. Marlowe, Christopher, 1564–1593. Doctor Faustus. 2. English drama–Early
modern and Elizabethan, 1500–1600—History and criticism. 3. Faust, -approxi-
mately 1540–In literature. I. Title.
   PR2664.L57 2016
   822'.3–dc23

Printed in China

Contents

Series Editors' Preface

The Shakespeare Handbooks provide an innovative way of studying the plays of Shakespeare and his contemporaries in performance. The commentaries, which are their core feature, enable a reader to envisage the words of a text unfurling in performance, involving actions and meanings not readily perceived except in rehearsal or performance. The aim is to present the plays in the environment for which they were written and to offer an experience as close as possible to an audience's progressive experience of a production.

While each book has the same range of contents, their authors have been encouraged to shape them according to their own critical and scholarly understanding and their first-hand experience of theater practice. The various chapters are designed to complement the commentaries: the cultural context of each play is presented together with quotations from original sources; the authority of its text or texts is considered with what is known of the earliest performances; key performances and productions of its subsequent stage history are both described and compared; an account is given of influential criticism of the play and the more significant is quoted extensively. The aim in all this has been to help readers to develop their own informed and imaginative view of a play in ways that supplement the provision of standard editions and are more userfriendly than detailed stage histories or collections of criticism from diverse sources.

We would like to acknowledge a special debt of gratitude to the founder of the Shakespeare Handbooks Series, John Russell Brown, whose energy for life, literature and theater we continue to find truly inspiring.

Paul Edmondson and Kevin Ewert

Preface

Of all non-Shakespearean plays from the early modern period, *Doctor Faustus* is probably the most widely read, anthologized, taught, and performed. Its story of a man selling his soul for knowledge and power has archetypal force, and has continued to recur in the literatures and mythologies of many subsequent cultures. Popular and influential in its own day, *Doctor Faustus* has great theatrical vitality, and has been successfully revived regularly in recent decades after centuries of relative obscurity. This book aims to illuminate some of the rich possibilities of *Doctor Faustus* as a play for performance.

The plot is simple and gripping. A scholar, John Faustus, dissatisfied with the traditional disciplines of philosophy, medicine, law, and theology, turns to magic in his quest for 'a world of profit and delight,/ Of power, of honour, of omnipotence.' He makes a bargain with Mephistopheles to bind his soul to Lucifer in return for 24 years of gratified desire. The years pass quickly, as Faustus's lofty aspirations give way to puerile pranks. As his end approaches, he conjures the shade of Helen of Troy to be his paramour, but can find no solace. He repeatedly considers repenting and turning to God, but is unable to do so. After a final hour of spiritual torment, he is taken to hell by devils, as the Chorus issues a final judgment: 'Cut is the branch that might have grown full straight.'

Part of what makes *Doctor Faustus* so compelling is its Janus-faced ambiguity, the complex and contradictory ways it presents its hero and his fateful bargain with the Devil. Readers, theatre-makers, and audiences have long grappled with interpretive questions about the play. Is it a parable about a justly damned sinner or a tragedy about a Promethean hero? Or is it perhaps a satirical critique of a theological system that denies free will? How do we reconcile the play's soaring poetry and knockabout comedy, its psychological terrors and firework-spouting devils? *Doctor Faustus* provides a potent theatrical experience, but audiences may leave the theatre wondering how to understand what they have seen and heard.

This ambiguity derives partly from the text itself, which exists in two different versions, with subtly different shades of meaning in their representation of Faustus's spiritual predicament. Ambiguity comes also from the complex figure of the play's author, and the times in which he lived. Christopher Marlowe was a divinity student, a poet, and a playwright, but also allegedly an atheist, a homosexual, and a spy. Any orthodox understanding of *Doctor Faustus* must contend with Marlowe's reputation for unorthodox belief. Further, early modern England was a dynamic period of religious controversy, scientific discovery, and imperial conquest. The expansive cultural energies of the time seem to be reflected in the striving, larger-than-life heroes who populate Marlowe's plays. The aspiring spirit of Faustus, the sensuous richness of his language, the psychological depth of his soliloquies, all seem too large to contain in a simple morality-play format. The contradictory impulses at work in *Doctor Faustus* are aptly, if oversimply, conveyed in an epigram attributed to the Oxford classicist R. M. Dawkins: Doctor Faustus is a Renaissance man who pays a medieval price.

Whatever *Doctor Faustus* might have meant in Marlowe's time, it remains compelling in our own. Modern audiences may not believe, as Marlowe's supposedly did, that real devils are appearing on the stage, but the play's diabolic hijinks can still be both frightening and entertaining. The play's comic scenes, long derided by scholars, prove their value in the theatre, provoking salutary laughter and ironic insight into Faustus's story. Mephistopheles's chilling assertion that 'this is hell, nor am I out of it,' has a stark horror, even in a secular context. And whether or not one believes in damnation, the play's harrowing account of unsatisfied longing, dubious bargain, and debilitating despair retains its force. Faustian bargains are still made every day, in areas ranging from employment to politics to personal relationships, as people choose to compromise one set of values in hope to gain in terms of another set. Such pacts still generally disappoint; the midnight hour always strikes. In the global twenty-first century, no less than in Marlowe's London, *Doctor Faustus* still resonates with a powerful question: '… what shall it profit a man, if he shall gain the whole world, and lose his own soul?' (Mark 8:36).

This volume is designed to help students of *Doctor Faustus* explore the play as a text for performance, to think about how it creates meaning in the theatre, whether in Marlowe's time or our own. The play demands that its interpreters, then or now, confront a series of critical questions. Why does Faustus abandon traditional learning and turn to 'cursèd necromancy'? Once he enters into his pact with Mephistopheles, why is he unable or unwilling to get out of it? How are Mephistopheles, the other devils, and the Seven Deadly Sins represented on the stage? How do the central scenes of comic trickery work in the overall design of the play, and what do they contribute to Faustus's spiritual trajectory? How is Helen of Troy represented? What are the theological implications, and emotional effects, of Faustus's final failure to repent? How are his last moments staged, and with what judgment is the audience invited to 'regard his hellish fall'? The following pages will consider how some of these questions might have been answered in Marlowe's time, and how they continue to be explored in our own.

I want to express my gratitude to Paul Edmondson for first involving me with this project, and to Rachel Bridgewater and the staff at Palgrave. I am deeply indebted to the previous scholarship on the play. Of particular importance for this volume have been the editions of David Bevington and Eric Rasmussen, as well as the Norton Critical Edition, edited by David Scott Kastan, and *Doctor Faustus: A Critical Guide*, edited by Sara Munson Deats. My thanks go to the archivists at the Shakespeare Centre Library, the Victoria and Albert Theatre and Performance Collection, Shakespeare's Globe, and Dulwich College. I am deeply grateful to my colleague Douglas Bruster for his collegial support and many helpful comments on the manuscript. I learned most of what I know about *Doctor Faustus* from my students in the University of Texas's Shakespeare at Winedale program, who performed the play in the summer of 2013. My thanks go to them, and particularly to Reagan Tankersley, who played Faustus and also proofread my initial draft. I want as always to thank my wife Laurel, who helped at every stage to bring this book to life. Finally, I want to thank my parents, who provided for me, among many other things, models of exemplary scholarship: to them the book is dedicated.

1 The Text and Early Performances

Texts and date

The textual history of *Doctor Faustus* is one of the most vexing problems in early modern theatre studies. The play exists in two distinct versions, both of which went through several editions. Neither was printed until more than a decade after Marlowe's death, and both were probably written, in part, by someone other than Marlowe.

Scholars refer to these two versions as the A-text and the B-text. The A-text was printed in 1604, the B-text in 1616. The A-text is relatively short, about 1500 lines; the B-text is more than 600 lines longer, and contains material for which there is no equivalent in the earlier text. In many scenes the texts are nearly identical, but there are significant divergences, and each contains material not in the other. We know that Philip Henslowe, who managed the theatre associated with early performances of the play, paid William Birde and Samuel Rowley £4 for 'additions in Doctor Faustus' in 1602, before either text was published. These 'additions' may or may not have been the new B-text material, but Henslowe's record of them indicates that the text of *Doctor Faustus* was a malleable and unstable entity while the play was being performed in the Elizabethan theatre.

The two texts are most similar in the opening and closing sequences, in which Faustus makes his initial pact with the Devil and is finally dragged off to hell. Both contain Faustus's rejection of traditional studies, summoning of Mephistopheles, pact with Lucifer, and entertainment by the Seven Deadly Sins; both also contain his eleventh-hour monologue and final destruction. The two versions are most different in the comic sequences in the middle part of the play. The B-text has an episode involving a rival German pope named

Bruno for which there is no equivalent in A. It also has a whole series of scenes depicting the vanquishing of a knight who questions Faustus's powers, an event that occupies only a few lines in the A-text. The comic subplot of the clowns who steal one of Faustus's conjuring books exists in different versions in the two texts, with the B-text's being substantially longer and including additional characters. The B-text also contains a larger presence for the supernatural characters, and includes an extra scene in which Faustus's fellow scholars discover his torn limbs after his death. Even in the passages that are similar in the two texts, subtle differences in wording suggest divergent interpretations of Faustus's damnation. Finally, the B-text contains more elaborate stage effects, and includes evidence of censorship relating to religious language.

Scholars have long argued about how these texts might have arisen, and which should be given priority. Some editors have favored the A-text, as earlier and less polluted by the interpolations of other hands. Others have argued for the fuller B-text, sometimes suggesting that A is a corrupted 'bad quarto,' a memorial reconstruction of the play by actors, perhaps reflecting changes made in performance. Many editors and theatrical producers have conflated the two texts, taking scenes or readings from each. More recent critical practice has been to treat the two texts independently, with each having an identity and authority of its own. The Revels Student Edition of the play, edited by David Bevington and Eric Rasmussen (on which the present study is based) includes both versions in parallel texts, making it possible to compare readings within a given scene. Other recent texts, such as the original 1993 Bevington/Rasmussen edition and the recent Norton Critical Edition (ed. David Scott Kastan), include both texts separately. There have also been a number of recent editions of one text or the other; but no one can now claim to present a definitive edition of Christopher Marlowe's *Doctor Faustus*.

It is unlikely that any text we have is entirely Marlowe's work, whether or not it includes the Birde/Rowley 'additions.' Other authors who might have had a hand in *Doctor Faustus* include Thomas Nashe, Thomas Dekker, and Henry Porter, a playwright who had been at Cambridge with Marlowe and had associations with the Admiral's Men. Elizabethan playwrights often worked collaboratively, or added material to the plays of others. Authors had little control over intellectual property rights, and both theatre companies and printers would try to get more mileage out of plays under their control by incorporating new material. The comic scenes in the middle section of *Doctor Faustus* have often been considered the work of a collaborator or reviser, out of keeping with the dignity of the main story of Faustus's bargain and his 'hellish fall.' The very first editor of the play, C. W. Dilke, complains in 1814 that 'the buffoonery and stupid humour of the second-rate characters are constantly intruding on our notice' (*Old English Plays*, Vol. 1, x, n.); yet Dilke seems to have thought it possible that Marlowe wrote them. In any event, the comic scenes are present, in some form, in both versions, and are clearly built into the design of the play. Apart from the scenes involving Robin the Clown, all of the comic episodes in the middle of *Doctor Faustus*, from the Pope to the horse-courser, are based on the same source as the rest of the play, *The English Faust Book*. Moreover, the comic scenes have a thematic importance. The middle section of the play depicts the degeneration of Faustus's aspirations through the 24 years of his bargain; the scenes with the clowns present a grotesque reflection of this debasement, and Faustus eventually meets them on their own level with his pranks on the horse-courser. Whoever wrote the middle scenes of *Doctor Faustus*, they are a necessary part of the play, which without them would really have only a beginning and an end.

The difficulties raised by the two texts of *Doctor Faustus* are compounded by uncertainties about the play's date. The first record of a performance is in 1594, when Philip Henslowe, the manager of the Rose playhouse, entered it in his 'Diary' or account-book, one of the leading sources for Elizabethan Theatre history. This performance was more than a year after Marlowe's death; *Doctor Faustus* was certainly written, and probably performed, well before. The earliest plausible date is around 1588–9, soon after Marlowe's initial success with the two parts of *Tamburlaine*. Apparent references to *Faustus* in other plays from the period, notably Robert Greene's *Friar Bacon and Friar Bungay* (probably 1589), argue for the earlier date. On the other hand, there is no record before 1592 of the publication of Marlowe's principal source, *The History of the Damnable Life and Deserved Death of Doctor John Faustus*, otherwise known as *The English Faust Book*. It is possible that Marlowe had access to a manuscript, or that there was a lost earlier edition. *The German Faust Book*, from which *The Damnable Life* derives, was published in 1587, but there is no evidence that

Marlowe knew it or could have read it in German. So while *Faustus* could have been written early in Marlowe's career or shortly before his death, there is no conclusive argument for either date. Scholars are divided between the two possible dates of 1588–9 and 1592, though the earlier date has been favored more recently.

As to the question of when and where *Doctor Faustus* was first performed, the evidence is equally inconclusive. It is unlikely that the September 1594 performance recorded in Henslowe's Diary was actually the first; Henslowe usually specified when a play performed by the Admiral's Men was a new work, and he did not do so in the case of *Faustus*. Other early modern texts refer to performances of *Faustus* at the Theatre in Shoreditch and at the Belsavage Inn, neither of which is likely to have taken place after 1590. It is also impossible to say who first performed the play, especially if one accepts the earlier date of 1588–9. The role of Faustus is strongly associated with Edward Alleyn, who was for years the leading player of the Admiral's Men, but in the late 1580s he was performing with another company, Lord Strange's Men. By the mid-1590s two pre-eminent companies had emerged: the Chamberlain's Men, led by the Burbage family, who performed at the Theatre and later the Globe; and the Admiral's Men, led by Henslowe and Alleyn, who played at the Rose. The Chamberlain's Men came to be associated with the works of Shakespeare, the Admiral's Men with those of Marlowe. The extent to which there was any official 'duopoly' in the London theatre has been much debated by historians, but these were the two leading companies by the time of the first performance of *Doctor Faustus* that we can document with certainty. While some other company may have performed it earlier, the play is primarily associated with the Admiral's Men, and the role of Faustus with Edward Alleyn.

Early performances

We know that the Admiral's Men produced *Doctor Faustus* at the Rose theatre on 30 September 1594, with Alleyn in the title role. The play brought in £3 and 12 shillings, an excellent box office taking. They continued to produce *Faustus* at regular intervals, 24 times over the next 3 years, when they pulled it from the repertoire because of Alleyn's temporary retirement from the stage. It remained a profitable piece for the Admiral's Men throughout this period (though the receipts declined over time), and was revived well into the seventeenth century. Henslowe's payment for additions to the text in 1602, and the number of print editions of the play, attest to its continuing popularity.

The Rose was in many ways characteristic of the public playhouses of the sixteenth century. It was located outside the City of London, just south of the Thames on the Bankside, near the site where Shakespeare's Globe would be built in 1599. Playhouses were typically situated in the 'liberties' outside the city limits, in part because of the anti-theatrical prejudices of puritanical civic authorities. Playhouses were a relatively new type of building in London; the Rose was only the fourth to be built, in 1587, shortly before Marlowe's *Tamburlaine* premiered there. Like other London public theatres, the Rose was a polygonal structure made from timber and stucco, with tiered audience galleries roofed with thatch, and a central yard open to the sky. At one side of the yard was a raised stage. Audience members sat in the galleries or stood in the yard to watch the performance.

The archeological remains of the Rose were discovered in 1989, revealing a wealth of information about this particular playhouse. The Rose was somewhat smaller than other London theatres, about 70 feet in diameter, though it still would have held up to 2000 spectators. In 1592 Henslowe undertook renovations on the Rose to increase its capacity, giving it an ovoid shape, opening out on the stage side. He also moved the stage back to further enlarge the yard, and probably added a roof or 'heavens' to protect the stage from the elements. This 'heavens' unit would also have contained machinery allowing for spectacular entries from above, such as the descent of the heavenly throne near the end of the B-text of *Faustus*.

At the back of the stage was the tiring house, from which the actors entered the space through two doors. There was probably also a curtained 'discovery space' or central alcove in which, for instance, Faustus could be seen seated in his study at the beginning of the play's first scene. This space may later have served for the hell-mouth into which Faustus was dragged, though he may also have descended through a trap-door in the stage itself. The Elizabethan stage had inherited a meaningful moral geography from medieval tradition. The heavens were above the stage, hell below, and humanity in the middle. This sense of the cosmic architecture of the Elizabethan stage is very strong in *Faustus*, so it is likely that performances employed the trap-door for demonic entrances and exits. The woodcut on the title page of the 1616 B-text shows a devil appearing to rise from a stage trap. On the other hand, the B-text also includes scenes in which supernatural agents seem to watch Faustus from above. They would likely have been standing in a gallery, or at a window, at the back of the stage. The B-text also has the mocking Benvolio '*Enter... above at a window.*' We know the Rose had such a second level because of its prominent use in Shakespeare's *Henry VI* plays, which also premiered there. The A-text does not specifically require a second level, which has led some to speculate that it represents a version of the play simplified for touring to different venues. However, it is likely that performances at the Rose, of whatever text, would have made use of this feature of the stage.

Performances of *Doctor Faustus* at the Rose would have taken place in the afternoon. Though some of the play's crucial scenes take place at night, performances would have been lit by natural daylight. The atmosphere of menace and mystery for a scene like Faustus's conjuring of Mephistopheles, or his final vigil before his midnight damnation, would have been created by other means than theatrical lighting. The language of these scenes does most of the work, along with theatrical effects like the tolling of the bell in 5.2. Early modern plays often signal night scenes by having actors carry props like torches or lanterns, but *Doctor Faustus* doesn't specifically call for these.

While Elizabethan outdoor theatres could do little in the matter of lighting, they certainly had special effects. Fireworks are specified several times in the performance of *Faustus*: when Mephistopheles summons a devil-wife for Faustus, when Faustus and Mephistopheles disrupt the Pope's banquet, when Mephistopheles frightens the clowns who have conjured him, and (in the B-text) when Benvolio and his followers are discomfited by a demonic army. Pyrotechnical effects would have been exciting for Elizabethan spectators, as well as downright dangerous in theatres made largely of wood (the Globe burned down in 1613 after the firing of a cannon ignited its thatched roof). Other special effects used in *Doctor Faustus* include the sound of thunder, the appearances of devils, and the processional entries of the Papal and Imperial courts. In general, the B-text calls for more elaborate uses of the stage, a larger company of actors, and more special effects; the A-text may reflect either a touring performance or a period when the company had fewer resources at its disposal.

The Admiral's Men

A typical Elizabethan playing company consisted of around a dozen or so actors, all male, plus boys to play the female roles and walk-on extras hired as needed. Both texts of *Doctor Faustus* require at least 11 actors, assuming the Seven Deadly Sins all appear onstage together with Faustus, Mephistopheles, Lucifer, and Beelzebub in 3.2. Though the play has a relatively large number of characters – more than 50 in the B-text – many of them appear only once or twice and then disappear, so doubling would have been relatively easy. The actors who played the Sins would have reappeared as the Pope and his retinue and the Emperor and his court, as well as the low-life characters in Act 4 and the devils who come for Faustus in Act 5. There are few female characters, so the effects of cross-gender casting would have been less pronounced than in other plays of the period, but still perhaps important. Helen of Troy, for instance, would have been played by a boy, so her kiss with Faustus might have contained a complicated erotic charge – perhaps especially if Marlowe's reputed homosexuality had been widely known.

While several scenes in *Doctor Faustus* make use of a large company that would have filled the small stage of the Rose, the largest share of the lines, and of stage time, belonged to only two actors, Faustus and Mephistopheles. We do not know who played Mephistopheles for the Admiral's Men, but he must have been a proficient and charismatic actor. The part is not huge from a line standpoint – Mephistopheles has around 170 lines in the A-text, a little over 10% of the play – but his presence is vital, even in the several scenes where he remains silent for long periods. Mephistopheles often has to match Faustus in tense encounters where Faustus does most of the talking, but Mephistopheles holds his own through a few concise, charged phrases: 'In hell.'; 'Under the heavens.'; 'I will not.'; 'Remember this.' There are of course a range of ways the role can be played, but in the early modern theatre it required an actor who could command attention through his silent presence and express magnetic power through often understated speech.

About the actor of Faustus, Edward Alleyn, we know a good deal more. He was the greatest tragic actor of his age, only eclipsed in his supremacy when Richard Burbage rose to pre-eminence in the plays of Shakespeare. Born in 1566, Alleyn would have been in his late 20s when he began playing Faustus. He retired from acting before he was 40, though he continued to be involved in theatre management and the sport of bear-baiting; he had a royal appointment as Master of the Bears. Wealthy from his career in the entertainment industry, Alleyn bought a manor house in Dulwich and endowed the College of God's Gift. Now Dulwich College, it is still one of the leading boys' schools in England and the repository of Alleyn and Henslowe's papers, the world's most important archive of Elizabethan Theatre history. Alleyn had a long and successful marriage to Henslowe's stepdaughter, and after her death he married the daughter of the poet and clergyman John Donne.

As an actor Alleyn was known for his imposing stature, power-ful voice, and commanding presence. He played all of Marlowe's leading parts, initially achieving fame as Tamburlaine, the Scythian conqueror who 'threaten[ed] the world with high astounding terms' in the two epic plays that bear his name (*Tamburlaine Part I*, Prologue, line 5). Alleyn gained something of a reputation for 'stalking and roaring,' as one contemporary described it, in Tamburlaine and similar roles. The classically minded Ben Jonson spoke disap-provingly of 'the scenical strutting, and furious vociferation' of Tamburlaine (*The Works of Ben Jonson*, Vol. 7, 95), and it seems likely that Hamlet's disdain for players who 'strutted and bellowed' may indicate Shakespeare's critique of Alleyn, and preference for Burbage's more naturalistic style. On the other hand, the perfor-mance by the First Player in *Hamlet*, which seems to be an homage to Alleyn's portrayal of Aeneas in Marlowe's *Dido, Queen of Carthage*, is powerful and moving; Hamlet praises it, while only the foolish Polonius finds it 'too long.' And it should also be remembered that Alleyn played other roles that required other sorts of attributes, including (probably) the grief-crazed Hieronymo in Kyd's *Spanish Tragedy*, the crafty Barabas in Marlowe's *Jew of Malta*, and Cleanthes, the comic master of disguise in Chapman's *Blind Beggar of Alexandria*. So while Alleyn had something of a reputation for ranting roles, they did not constitute the limit of his abilities. He seems to have had a sense of humor about this aspect of his dramatic persona; in a family letter he jokes about being a 'fustian king' (fustian is fabric padding and, metaphorically, overstuffed rhetoric). Some of Alleyn's signature style no doubt came through in the role of Faustus. The horse-courser refers to him as 'Doctor Fustian.'

A portrait of Alleyn at Dulwich depicts him as tall and handsome in middle age, soberly gowned, with expressive hazel eyes, long prominent nose, and a broad chestnut-colored beard. An engraving of the younger Alleyn as Tamburlaine is less detailed, but shows the same features, with long hair and an elegant doublet and cloak. His costume for Faustus may have combined these two styles. The Henslowe/Alleyn papers include a detailed inventory of Alleyn's costumes, which lists 'Faustus Jerkin his cloak' as the last of his 17 'Jerkins and Doublets.' 'Jerkin' suggests a shorter garment like a doublet, but 'cloak' could be some sort of long scholar's gown. A 1609 satire by Samuel Rowlands called *The Knave of Clubs* includes lines that refer to Alleyn's costume for the role:

> The gull gets on a surplice,
> With a cross upon his breast,
> Like Alleyn playing Faustus,
> In that manner he was dressed.

> (*The Collected Works of Samuel Rowlands*, (Glasgow, 1880), II, 29)

Rowlands's lines suggest that Faustus's costume had a distinctly religious appearance to it, not out of character for a scholar but deeply ironic given the trajectory of the character.

Alleyn had an outstanding memory, for he played Faustus in repertory with *The Jew of Malta* and *Tamburlaine* – all demanding roles of great length. He was onstage for virtually the entirety of *Doctor Faustus*, absent only from the brief comic scenes, and beginning and ending the play with long monologues. Though he was successful in the role – the play was the chief moneymaker for the Admiral's Men during the period from 1594–7 – references to the play in performance chiefly focus on something else: the supernatural aspects. Elizabethan audiences seem to have loved *Doctor Faustus*, but were a little afraid of it. With its scenes of conjuring, multiple devils and spirits, and spectacular descent into hell, *Doctor Faustus* created an atmosphere of terror that spawned a number of enduring theatrical legends.

Several different seventeenth-century anecdotes mention super-natural happenings during performances of *Doctor Faustus*. The 1604 play *The Black Book* refers to someone who 'had a head of hair like one of my devils in *Doctor Faustus* when the old Theatre cracked and frighted the audience.' (Kastan, 180) This account may only refer to a planned special effect, such as thunder or pyrotechnics, but it conveys the play's power to startle. William Prynne, in the 1633 anti-theatrical tract *Histrio-mastix*, mentions:

> the visible apparition of the devil on the stage at the Belsavage playhouse, in Queen Elizabeth's days, to the great amazement both of the actors and spectators, whiles they were there profanely playing the History of Faustus, the truth of which I have heard from many now alive, who well remember it, there being some distracted with that fearful sight.

The idea that the play's black magic had the power to summon actual devils occurs repeatedly in these stories. The most elaborate account, a handwritten note in an Elizabethan book, is of a touring perfor-mance in Exeter:

> As Faustus was busy in his magical invocations, on a sudden they were all dashed, every one harkening other in the ear, for they were all persuaded there was one devil too many amongst them; and so after a little pause desired the people to pardon them, they could go no farther with this matter. The people also understanding the thing as it was, every man hastened to be first out of doors. The players, as I heard it, contrary to their custom spend-ing the night in reading and prayer, got them out of town the next morning.

Finally, John Aubrey, the Restoration-era chronicler of *Brief Lives*, mentions a similar story about Alleyn himself, though he mistakenly attributes the play to Shakespeare. Aubrey attributes Alleyn's found-ing of Dulwich College to the fright he received from the incident. For the most part these are merely entertaining anecdotes, but they do communicate something about the fear the play could arouse – and suggest that this fear was part of the reason for its popularity. The increase in spectacular supernatural effects between the A- and B-texts, and in adaptations of the play through the seventeenth century, reinforces the notion that what audiences responded to in *Faustus* was its transgressive trafficking in the demonic, and the spec-tacles, theatrical or supernatural, that this might produce.

But if *Doctor Faustus* is partly a diabolical conjuring show, it is also many other things. It is a serious theological reflection on the nature of temptation and the possibility of salvation. It is a classically styled tragedy about the fall of a Promethean hero whose 'waxen wings did mount above his reach.' It is one of the masterworks of a supreme lyric poet of the English Renaissance, whose sensual imagery and 'mighty line' grace its most celebrated passages. And it is a monument of early modern stagecraft, marshaling the resources of the theatre of its time in ways that remain utterly compelling more than 400 years later. The commentary that follows will explore the power and possibilities of *Doctor Faustus* in performance, then and now.

2 Commentary: The Play in Performance

Like any play, *Doctor Faustus* exists only partly on the page of a printed book. It was written for performance, and in performance it takes on a rich and complicated life. Countless decisions that go into staging a play: the casting of roles; inflection of lines; movement of actors; choice of costumes, properties, music, and special effects. In *Doctor Faustus* these staging decisions range from broad interpretive questions about the meaning of Faustus's damnation to technical challenges like the representation of the Seven Deadly Sins. And even when all of these decisions are made, each performance still unfolds differently in the live, intimate communication of actors and audience.

The situation is even more complicated in *Doctor Faustus*, which exists in two different versions, as discussed in the first chapter. While current critical practice treats the two texts as separate and distinct, the theatre has always made free use of whatever material was available, as the history of Marlowe's play shows. Accordingly, the following commentary will make reference to both the 1604 and 1616 versions, known as the A- and B-texts. References are to the Revels Student Edition, which prints the two texts on facing pages. Line numbering will generally follow the A-text, which will be the primary text throughout; but where the B-text offers significantly different options, these will also be considered. The order and numbering of scenes follows the Revels edition. The A-text does not number the scenes, but I have followed the act and scene numbers that the Revels editors have derived from B, to make it easier to reference both texts.

This commentary will explore some of the performance possibilities of *Doctor Faustus*, and the way they can generate a wide range of meanings from this remarkable play. I will consider both the conventions of the Elizabethan theatre and the possibilities available to contemporary production. The commentary will direct attention to such performance elements as movement, gesture, and stage position; to vocal effects such as inflection, volume, emphasis, and direction of speech; and to the visual aspects of costume and *mise-en-scène*. I will also consider the special effects involved in the highly theatrical moments of supernatural spectacle, which were clearly a part of *Doctor Faustus*'s appeal for an early modern audience. I comment on interpretive cruxes within the action, calling attention to places where different ways of playing a line or scene can lead to very different understandings of the play's overall meaning. The goal is not to define some ideal production, but rather to help the reader understand how the play unfolds in performance, moment by moment. By consulting this commentary in conjunction with a reading of the play, the reader will, I hope, develop a sense of the theatrical richness and vitality that make Marlowe's *Doctor Faustus* one of the greatest plays of the early modern theatre.

Prologue

In both the A- and B-texts, *Doctor Faustus* begins with a prologue, spoken by the Chorus. Such prologues were not the norm in the Elizabethan theatre, but neither were they uncommon. While only about 40% of all early modern plays had prologues, they were popular in Marlowe's day, and four of his seven plays have them. A prologue could serve a number of formal functions: introducing the subject matter of the play, appealing for the audience's attention and indulgence, perhaps distinguishing a particular play from the general tendencies of the drama of the day. The prologue to *Doctor Faustus* does all of these.

The speaker is identified simply as Chorus. In Marlowe's theatre he may have worn conventional trappings associated with such a role – a black gown and a laurel wreath – or he may have been costumed as one of the characters the actor would go on to portray in the performance proper. The A-text attributes a choral-sounding speech to Wagner, and it is possible the two roles may have been shared by one actor, or even conflated. Many modern productions have had Wagner speak the lines of the Chorus. The role also offers opportunities for non-traditional casting, in a play with few women's parts. When William Poel revived the play in 1896, he had a classically dressed female Chorus, complete with laurel wreath, and several subsequent productions have followed his lead.

The Chorus's entrance may have been preceded by a trumpet fanfare or other musical introduction appropriate to the tone of the play. It is possible that the stage was draped with black cloth to indicate the performance of a tragedy. The Chorus presumably entered from a door or curtain at the back, walked to the center of the stage, and addressed the audience directly.

1–6 The language of the prologue is some of the most characteristic of the richly elevated, grandiloquent style we think of as 'Marlovian.' With exotic polysyllabic names like 'Trasimene' and 'Carthaginians,' and densely modified phrases like 'proud audacious deeds' and 'learning's golden gifts,' the prologue has the grandeur and sonority to fit the aspiring Renaissance spirit. A number of regular pentameters have the ringing cadences of Marlowe's 'mighty line.' The speech has little enjambment, and often builds up its sentences through multiple parallel and end-stopped phrases, as in the opening six lines. The types of plays from which the Chorus distinguishes *Doctor Faustus* sound rather like others that Marlowe wrote: marching and battles are subjects of *Tamburlaine, Dido* features Carthaginians, and *Edward II* (probably written after *Faustus*) would explore states overturned through the dalliance of kingly love.

7–10 One choice that any production will have to make is the pronunciation of the hero's name, which occurs over 150 times. Does the first syllable of Faustus rhyme with 'house' or 'cost'? The former choice, using the same vowel sound as the German 'Faust,' has become standard in the US and increasingly common in the UK. But a pronunciation corresponding to Henslowe's 'Fostes' used to be the norm, and is still often heard in Britain. The phrase 'the form of Faustus's fortunes' may suggest a repetition of similar sounds.

In appealing for the audience's approval, the Chorus refers back to the traditions of the classical theatre; the word 'plaud' in the A-text suggests the appeal for applause ('*Plaudite*') at the end of a Roman comedy. In addressing the audience as 'gentlemen' (or 'gentles',

B-text), the Chorus perhaps flatters the audience slightly and builds a sense of community.

11–27 The middle section of the prologue briefly recounts Faustus's biography, using the scant details available from *The English Faust Book*. Much of the language is heavily moralizing, employing stark polarities of good and evil, contrasting the 'sweet' and 'heavenly' delights of theology with the 'devilish exercise' of 'cursèd necromancy.' But the prominent image of lines 20–2, an allusion to the classical story of Icarus, allows for a more complex response to Marlowe's overreaching hero. Though admonitory, the reference to Icarus' flying too close to the sun with his waxen wings may suggest an ambitious striving with which the audience is invited, at some level, to sympathize. Moreover, the notion that the heavens 'conspired' his overthrow may resonate with later scenes in which Faustus proves unable to repent. The B-text, in particular, may support the notion of a supernatural conspiracy against the protagonist.

28 The prologue ends with the Chorus directing the audience's attention to Faustus in his study. At the Rose playhouse in 1594, Faustus was presumably revealed in the 'discovery space' at the back of the stage. Perhaps the Chorus drew open a curtain; in the modern theatre Faustus may be illuminated by a light change. At any rate, Faustus initially appears seated at his desk, the iconic image of a scholar, just as Barabas in *The Jew of Malta* is discovered in his countinghouse. As in the B-text title page illustration, Faustus may be surrounded by such emblems of learning as a globe or astrolabe, or at least the books that figure so prominently in his opening monologue.

Act I

Act I, scene i

The first scene of the play shows Faustus rejecting other branches of learning to devote himself to magic. For more than half the scene Faustus is alone onstage, considering his future course or reveling in the powers he will attain. These moments provide a prime opportunity for the leading actor to characterize Faustus and introduce him to the audience. In the original production this would have been Edward Alleyn, the leading player of the Admiral's Men and an actor celebrated for his charisma and vocal power. Faustus's long first speech establishes his aspiring spirit and self-confidence, as well as his academic achievements. But room remains for actorly interpretation. Is Faustus a rebellious seeker after truth, or a self-serving sensualist and egomaniac? Elements of both can come through in this first scene, as Faustus develops his plans and then meets with the magicians who will help him realize them.

1–5 Faustus's soliloquy begins with a firm self-address. The imperative mood, and the counter-metrical stress on the first syllable of his first word, gives Faustus's opening speech force and purpose. The determination to be a divine 'in show,' however, lends an edge of underhandedness and cynicism to the confident tone. Furthermore, while the first line turns on the word 'begin,' the word 'end' occurs repeatedly throughout the speech (meaning goal, but carrying other associations implying finality, death, and so forth).

The actor may move out of his study enclosure and speak directly to the audience, though most of his words are in fact addressed to himself, or to the books that stand in for various academic disciplines.

6–12 This extended monologue, the play's longest speech, repeats a pattern in which Faustus considers and rejects the diverse branches of medieval learning. Each subject is represented by a particular book, and illustrated by one or more quotations in Latin or Greek. The classical languages give an impressively learned sound to the speech, though Faustus responds to each quotation in a way that effectively provides an English translation. Logic, represented by Aristotle, is the first study to be rejected.

Faustus's curt dismissal, along with his reference to himself in the third person, conveys his pride and arrogance. Throughout the play, Faustus frequently refers to himself by name, often in second-person self-exhortations such as that of the speech's first line.

13–26 As with logic, Faustus dismisses medicine through the use of rhetorical questions: here a series of three, with the third extending over three lines. The details about his medical accomplishments briefly flesh out our sense of Faustus's history and achievements. His recognition that he is 'still but Faustus, and a man,' suggests a moment of reflection, one of the sobering hints of mortality that give gravity to Faustus from time to time throughout the play. His dissatisfaction with medicine, as subject to physical laws and the mortal limits of human life, hints at his Promethean ambitions.

27–36 Faustus next rejects a legal career (the A-text's 'church' in line 33 is evidently a mistake; the B-text reads 'law' at this point). Faustus's haughty contempt for this 'mercenary' profession reflects his lofty ideals at this point, ideals that will shortly come into question. Two of his Latin quotations end in '*et cetera*'; if the actor actually speaks this word aloud, it can contribute to the sense of Faustus's weary disenchantment with traditional studies.

37–50 In considering theology, Faustus may have moments of serious reflection – his 'Ha!' could be a flash of awareness or a cynical laugh – but the overall tone is cavalier, marked by short, offhand phrases such as 'That's hard,' '*Che serà, serà,*' and 'Divinity, adieu!' Such moments often generate laughter in performance. The lengthy Latin quotations, and their translations, violate the blank verse structure of the speech and possibly send it into prose for lines 44–7 (editors set these lines in different ways, but they are certainly irregular in length and rhythm). Tellingly, Faustus omits those aspects of the scriptural passages that promise salvation for repentant sinners. Elizabethan theatregoers, accustomed to hearing scripture quoted in sermons, might well have noted these omissions. They begin the important motif of Faustus's spiritual blindness and hard-heartedness, which runs through the play.

51–65 Having rejected the other subjects – perhaps tossing aside the volumes representing them – Faustus turns to the 'necromantic books' that are his real interest. How the actor handles and responds to the various books is a key bit of business in the scene. He may retrieve the necromantic books from a secret hiding place, and treat them differently from the others. Books are among the most important properties of the play, and Faustus's magic books should be distinctive and impressive.

Faustus's paean to magic alters the rhythm of the speech. After the relative flatness of the earlier dismissals, his language opens out into broader thoughts and rolling phrases. The expansiveness of the verse comes through in grand polysyllabic words ('metaphysics,' 'necromantic,' 'omnipotence'), in longer sentences, and in the use of five-item lists. The practices of magic take on an incantatory quality at line 53, and the fruits of occult studies, separated by the repeated preposition 'of,' give a rising, striving quality to lines 55–6. This distinctive rhetoric of aspiration is used by many of Marlowe's heroes, and it gives a swelling emotional lift to the final section of Faustus's opening monologue.

66–71 Wagner's immediate appearance in response to Faustus's summons creates the first character interaction of the play. Wagner's promptness may be comic or ominous, in keeping with the range of possible interpretations of this important supporting character, who serves variously as a comic drudge, a magus-in-training, and an almost choral figure documenting Faustus's career. He is probably recognizable as a servant from his costume, though this could suggest anything from a butler to a lab assistant.

72–9 Two supernatural characters – identified as the Good and Evil Angels in the A-text, and the '*Angel and Spirit*' in B – enter, probably through opposite doors, and make their appeals to Faustus. The Good and Evil Angels connect *Doctor Faustus* to the medieval morality play tradition, with their *psychomachia*, or battle over Faustus's soul. Their first appearance affords an opportunity for expressive costuming and theatrical magic. Their equivalent, but contrasting, four-line speeches suggest the way these characters are both paired and opposite. Though this first entrance is brief, it probably created a *frisson* of nervous excitement in the early modern audience; anecdotal evidence suggests that the appearance of supernatural or demonic characters on the stage in this play engendered a good deal of anxiety among spectators. Renaissance audiences would have immediately understood their symmetrical appeals, and the image is still one we recognize, in parodic form, from cartoons and comic movies. For the RSC in 1974, Ian McKellen famously used hand puppets and spoke the lines of the angels himself, making the *psychomachia* a purely internal debate.

80–99 Faustus rhapsodizes over the powers and achievements magic will bring. The Renaissance thirst for knowledge, power, wealth, and sensual experience, well established in Marlowe's other heroes, here finds its fullest expression. The speech mixes invocations of the rich ('gold,' 'orient pearl') and the strange ('India,' 'the new-found world,' 'strange philosophy') with images of physical pleasure ('pleasant fruits ... princely delicates ... silk') and plans for political dominion. Even Faustus's image for military power – a burning ship employed in a recent low-countries' conflict – has a foreign, exotic grandeur about it, and Faustus's new weapons will be even 'stranger' than that.

100–20   Faustus repeats the names of his fellow magicians four and five times in the scene. This repetition may betoken awe or flattery on Faustus's part, but it certainly reveals Marlowe's fondness for euphonious proper names. Faustus briefly rehearses his rejections of philosophy, law, medicine, and divinity, heaping robust contempt on the last (though the lines condemning divinity are absent from the B-text, perhaps because of censorship). The last part of the speech invokes something of Faustus's early career and notoriety, employing allusions to legend and literature, as well as further exotic names, in his references to Musaeus and Agrippa.

121–50   Valdes and Cornelius may simply be other Scholars, attired similarly to Faustus; or they may have something of the supernatural in their demeanor. Their speeches are equivalent in length and formally similar, and they are likely to take up symmetrical positions on either side of Faustus as they woo him with 'the miracles that magic will perform' and their material rewards. Valdes's speech is especially rich poetically. It reflects Marlowe's geographical interests, as well as early modern political realities, in references to Spanish conquest, 'Indian Moors,' 'Lapland giants,' and 'Almain rutters,' but it takes on some of the qualities of Marlowe's Ovidian love poetry in the lyrically sensual image of line 129–31. The twinned speeches' allure encompasses power, beauty, knowledge, and the exotic, a panoply of Renaissance motivations.

151–68   Faustus has been determined on his course since before the entry of the magicians, so at this stage there is no clear decision point committing him to the black arts. Rather, the remainder of the scene builds anticipation about the upcoming conjuring, with repeated words pointing toward the end of the present scene and the actions soon to come: 'Come ... haste thee ... first ... ere I sleep ... this night.' The scene probably closes with a bustling exit, perhaps into the space representing Faustus's study, as the magicians go to dinner.

Act I, scene ii

The next scene serves to pass the time before Faustus's conjuring of Mephistopheles, and to give a sense of his separation from the community of scholars. It also offers a change of pace and tone, with mocking prose comedy replacing the elevated verse of the earlier scene.

The alternation of verse and prose – the latter often, though not always, used for characters of lower status and scenes of comedy – was a structural feature of Elizabethan drama. Douglas Bruster, in 'Christopher Marlowe and the Verse/Prose Bilingual System,' has argued that Marlowe was the principal architect of this important convention. Of Marlowe's plays, *Doctor Faustus* contains by far the highest percentage of prose – nearly half of the A-text and more than a third of B. It appears primarily in comic scenes like 1.2 and 1.4, but also in several other contexts throughout the play, as will be noted.

1–18 Two Scholars enter, presumably recognizable from their black robes or other academic regalia, and accost Wagner, who enters from the other door carrying wine. The Scholars, who return to serve as foils to Faustus at the end of the play, are the voice of conventional piety and morality. As such, they may be played as gravely dignified or somewhat pompous figures, but certainly they are susceptible to Wagner's irreverent wit. It is noteworthy that Wagner is described as Faustus's 'boy'; though this may be largely a comment on his social status (and presumably Wagner, like Faustus, ages 24 years over the course of the action). In this scene Wagner shows the insouciance of the wily servant figure from classical comedy or *commedia dell'arte*, using hair-splitting logic to fend off the Scholars' enquiries about Faustus.

19–32 Just as the frustrated Scholars are ready to give up on him, Wagner promises to provide information. He launches into a parody of academic discourse that allows him to mock the Scholars further, using rhetorical questions, fragments of Latin, and – perhaps not incidentally – references to two of the Seven Deadly Sins that will appear later. Wagner archly uses the figure of epanorthosis, or self-correction, to change 'lechery' to 'love' – a cynical moment that will likely draw an audience laugh. He protests that he is 'slow to wrath,' but he perhaps becomes a little menacing, rather than merely pert, in the middle of the speech. His raillery takes on an aggressive tone with his jests about hanging. For the last part of his speech, Wagner adopts the preaching manner of a 'precision' or Puritan, and then undercuts it with the bathetic, long-delayed news that Faustus is within at dinner.

33–40 After Wagner's jokey exit, the scene takes a more serious tone as the Scholars express concern for Faustus. Even if they have been made ridiculous in the preceding encounter, their lines now establish both Faustus's danger and their sympathy for him, and foreshadow their role in the final scenes.

Act I, scene iii

Faustus's initial conjuration of Mephistopheles provides a signature moment of demonic spectacle. The conversation that follows establishes the Faustus/Mephistopheles relationship. It contains searching and poignant dialogue about heaven, hell, and spiritual longing. It also extends the pattern whereby Faustus ignores warnings about the fate of his soul, and pushes forward on his course toward damnation.

1–7 The A-text stage direction reads merely '*Enter Faustus to conjure*'; the B-text specifies '*Thunder*' and the entry of '*Lucifer and four devils,*' though these play no obvious role in the scene. If the devils are visible throughout, for instance in the gallery space above the stage, their presence may suggest a powerful supernatural conspiracy against Faustus, and diminish the sense of his free will. The setting is presumably the 'solitary grove' mentioned in 1.1; *The English Faust Book* specifies 'a thick wood near to Wittenberg.' However, no scene change would have been likely in Marlowe's theatre.

Faustus enters bearing one or more books and the holy water he will use in his conjuration. The opening lines create an eerie atmosphere of night and fog. On the Elizabethan stage, the scene would have occurred in daylight, though some sort of smoke effects might have been possible.

8–15 In some manner Faustus creates a circle, perhaps merely tracing it on the stage with a staff, perhaps unfurling a painted floorcloth, perhaps doing something more exotic like dropping sand or ashes. If anything is actually painted or scattered on the stage, it is probably removed at the end of the scene, though the clowns in the following scene could help with the cleanup as part of their business. Alternatively, the circle could remain on the stage as a reminder of the initial conjuration. The title page woodcut from the B-text quarto shows Faustus conjuring in his study, with a small circle, covered with zodiacal symbols, on the floor around his feet, but not under them. If this image reflects stage practice, the circle may have been an easily removable prop.

Faustus's conjuration begins with a description of the circle's attributes, expressed in fairly regular, end-stopped verse. The single sentence builds through six even lines, adding mystery and grandeur to the moment with references to heavenly bodies and divine figures, and deploying the impressive, mouth-filling word 'anagrammatised.' Lines 14–15 raise the possibility of Faustus's fear, but overcome it with his determination to be 'resolute,' a word which, along with its verbal form 'resolve,' occurs several times in relation to Faustus.

16–20　From English verse Faustus switches to Latin prose for his conjuration. The change to Latin creates an atmosphere of learning and religious ritual; Marlowe's dramaturgy often exploits sound as well as sense. On the other hand, the content of these lines is such that even audience members without a classical education are likely to pick up on at least some of the meaning. There are direct cognates such as '*spiritus*,' '*inferni*,' and '*monarcha*'; the names of the four elements may be recognizable; and the proper names of Jehovah, Lucifer, and so on certainly will be. The conjuration builds to a climax with the name '*Mephistopheles*' at line 20 – but then there is a moment of (potentially comic) anticlimax as no devil arrives.

21–5　Faustus's continuation of the conjuring ends again with Mephistopheles's name, and this time a devil does appear, in some terrible form that Faustus rejects as 'too ugly.' On Marlowe's stage it may have arisen through the trap: the B-text illustration shows a devil coming up out of the floor. It is likely – based on the *Faust Book* source, an enigmatic B-text stage direction, and a reference in Henslowe's Diary – that the Devil was in the form of a dragon. Modern directors will likely make the most of this opportunity for spectacle; since the

Devil appears only momentarily and has no need to speak, the production can go all out for a memorable and frightening effect.

26–35 Faustus makes a sardonic anti-Catholic joke in charging Mephistopheles to return in the 'holy shape' of a Franciscan friar. However, Faustus seems unconscious of a similar irony as he congratulates himself on the power of his 'heavenly words.' The ironies continue as Faustus gloats over Mephistopheles's obedience and the force of his own spells; he will shortly have his assumptions challenged.

36–55 Mephistopheles's entrance introduces the play's second most important character. The interpretive range this role offers the actor is perhaps even greater than that of Faustus. He may be a smooth manipulator, an urbane and courtly companion, a frightening demon, or a tortured lost soul; very often he is some combination of all of these. Some recent productions have developed a homo-erotically charged relationship between Faustus and Mephistopheles; others, perhaps responding to the paucity of female parts, have used a female actor in the role. However Mephistopheles is characterized, his relationship with Faustus is intense and important.

His appearance, at least initially, must match that of a Franciscan friar, in a rough brown or grey, hooded habit and a white rope belt. There may be something supernatural or inhuman about his makeup or demeanor; on the other hand, his first entrance is presumably meant to contrast with the noisy and frightening devil that appeared before. Mephistopheles's gravity and restraint may be chilling in themselves. His first line seems simple and deferential, though it may contain a note of challenge. On the whole, he seems quite at ease in his early speeches, carefully explaining the reasons for his presence in ways that should serve as a warning to Faustus, but only call forth his arrogant assurance. The power dynamic between Faustus and Mephistopheles is constantly shifting, and provides much of the play's most complex drama. Ironically, Mephistopheles here uses some of the play's most explicitly Christian language, referring directly to God, the scriptures, the 'Saviour Christ,' the 'glorious soul,' and the Trinity.

56–64 Faustus's speech begins with a fourteen-beat line in the A-text, which modern editors often divide in two; either way it provides a contrast to the prevailing blank verse. The actor of Faustus could use this contrast to convey a change of attitude. Two short lines could betoken momentary hesitation on Faustus's part, whereas a smooth long line might suggest blustery confidence. His references to Elysium and 'the old philosophers' associate Faustus with the intellectual traditions of the Renaissance and its classical humanist worldview; but his dismissal of questions about the soul as 'vain trifles' would have sounded hubristic to an Elizabethan audience.

65–77   Faustus now opens a series of six questions and answers that recalls the Christian catechism; their quick back-and-forth rhythm also suggests the stichomythia of classical tragedy. Mephistopheles's answers to these questions – about Lucifer and the spirits who dwell with him – begin as terse single lines, then gradually expand into speeches of two, three, and seven lines. They also move from simple information, as in line 65, to more emotional content, including quite frank warnings about the spirits' past sins and present sufferings. Marlowe powerfully uses the rhetorical device of epistrophe, ending four successive lines with the name Lucifer, driving home the consequences of the fallen angels' commitment to their leader. After setting up this pattern in the blank verse, Marlowe breaks it with the simplicity of Faustus's blunt question and Mephistopheles's two-word answer, 'In hell.' The deflating effect can be comic, but it also sets up the chilling discussion that follows.

78–84   In one of the play's most famous speeches, Mephistopheles details his damnation. The first line, 10 simple monosyllables, is hair-raising in its matter-of-factness. Mephistopheles speaks calmly but with icy clarity about the fact that he is at that moment in hell. The rest of the speech builds in emotional intensity, to the point that Mephistopheles seems to be warning Faustus away from the damnation he has come to procure. Mephistopheles's memories of heaven have an almost sensual quality of longing – seeing the face of God, tasting the eternal joys – which is starkly contrasted by the hyperbole of 'ten thousand hells' and the contempt for Faustus's 'frivolous demands.' These lines could be played as some sort of reverse-psychology temptation, but they seem like a genuine expression of torment and warning. However played, this will be a key speech for any actor developing the role of Mephistopheles.

85–103 Faustus's response continues his hubristic arrogance. His cavalier dismissal of Mephistopheles's 'passionate' outcry, and his commendation of his own 'manly fortitude,' create a deep sense of irony for the audience. Faustus's attitude embodies a kind of courage, and confidence in human powers and abilities, that reflects Renaissance humanist optimism. Yet his insensitivity to the anguish Mephistopheles has related suggests both a coarseness of spirit and a crippling lack of foresight. His lines make clear that he understands the nature of his bargain for 'eternal death,' but he seems unable fully to comprehend its consequences. In line 92, the sibilant consonance of repeated s-sounds creates a sense of menace culminating in the bell-tolling ending on the word 'soul.' Faustus's selection of 'four and twenty years' for the period of his contract is inherited from the *Faust Book* source, but provides the actor interesting choices. Is the number selected arbitrarily and offhandedly, or with any forethought and foreboding? If dwelled upon, the number 24 may suggest the hours in a single day, and by extension, that final hour which the play is to dramatize so vividly later on.

Faustus's desire to live 'in all voluptuousness' invokes a sensuality that recurs from time to time, but which never seems to occupy Faustus's attention for long. Faustus spends more time dwelling on the services Mephistopheles will provide him. His use of anaphora, or repetition of initial words, creates a parallel in lines 96–8 between the desires for acquisition, knowledge, and power. The speech concludes with the last of 10 mentions of the name of Lucifer, six of these occurring as the final word of the line (the name Faustus also occurs 10 times in this short scene, Mephistopheles eight times). The last lines highlight Marlowe's penchant for alliteration, with seven m-sounds in the space of two lines.

104–16 After Mephistopheles exits, Faustus's final speech seems to constitute a ringing celebration of his bargain and the powers it will bring him. On the other hand, an actor could play the lines as a somewhat forced justification in the face of nagging doubts. The astronomical hyperbole of the first two lines is followed by an ambitious catalog of the projects Faustus plans to undertake. These comprise both geographical dominion – the speech combines the specific place names 'Africa,' 'Spain,' and 'Germany' with such topographical terms as 'ocean,' 'hills,' 'shore,' and 'land' – and scientific innovation. Faustus seems to propose some form of military air travel, as well as a civil engineering project to close off the Strait of Gibraltar. These projects, however, unlike those mentioned in 1.1, are all conceived, not in the spirit of the public good, but to increase Faustus's own lordly power (as lines 111–13 make clear). The speech ends on a slightly diminuendo note, as Faustus settles into self-satisfied contemplation as he awaits Mephistopheles's return.

Act I, scene iv

The comic scenes in *Doctor Faustus* have often been derided as clumsy additions by an inferior hand, but they clearly add something to the overall design of the play. Faustus's tragic trajectory is set against a series of oafish pranks and mean-spirited conjuring tricks, in which Faustus himself eventually participates. The short comic interlude of 1.4, though perhaps not written by Marlowe, provides an ironic counterpoint to the lofty aspirations of Faustus in the preceding scene. His servant Wagner, now having possessed himself of some limited magical powers of his own, uses them to terrorize a rustic clown and bring him into his service. The scene replicates the Faustus/Mephistopheles relationship on a lower plane, and introduces the theme of the degradation of Faustus's magic that will be a feature of subsequent comic episodes.

1–14   Having established Wagner as an insolent comic servant in 1.2, the play now provides him with a comic underling of his own. The Clown introduced here – presumably recognizable as such by the threadbare garments the text references – may or may not be the same character named as Robin in 2.2 and following scenes. In 2.2 Robin appears as an ostler at an inn where Faustus is staying, whereas the 1.4 Clown seems a rustic vagabond, so there is some justification for keeping the characters separate. But Occam's Razor and the economies of casting would both argue for treating them as the same character, and many modern texts assign the name Robin to the figure named only as Clown in both the A and B versions of this scene. The A-text scene is slightly longer and linguistically richer – for instance, the Clown refers to 'pickedevants' instead of the more pedestrian 'beards' of the B-text – but the two scenes are basically identical. The essential situation of a servant exercising petty despotism over one even lower than he is established immediately in both versions. Wagner's language is inflated, with a hint of the pseudo-puritanical haughtiness he displayed earlier ('how poverty jesteth in his nakedness'), as well as a sprinkling of schoolboy Latin. The Clown, by contrast, evinces a mixture of lumpen stupidity, low cunning, and lasciviousness ('mutton' was a term for prostitute, and several of the Clown's statements employ similar double entendres). The reference to giving one's soul to the Devil for a paltry return, of course, recalls Faustus's bargain.

15–44 Wagner's attempt to dragoon the Clown into his service for a period of 7 years likewise recalls the Faustus/Mephistopheles relationship, though with some ironic differences: in Faustus's case, though he is the one entering into the bond, Mephistopheles is the one acting as a servant. The Clown's situation is more straightforwardly disadvantageous; for briefly accepting a purse of coins, he is bound to Wagner and threatened with devilish torments if he breaks his articles. At line 43 Wagner implicates the audience by calling them to witness that the Clown did indeed accept the money; there may be comic business with tossing the coins back and forth. There is perhaps an element of social commentary here, glancing at the situation of impressed soldiers or indentured apprentices in Elizabethan England, but the overall tone remains one of ironic comedy.

45–76 The scene takes a surprising turn when Wagner is indeed able to conjure up a pair of devils to frighten the Clown. The frequent appearance of demons onstage seems to have been part of *Doctor Faustus*'s appeal, and these semi-comic devils provide both terror and humor. 'Balliol and Belcher,' as Wagner identifies them (the Clown can never get their names right), are probably recognizable as male and female – though in Marlowe's theatre both, of course, would have been male actors. The Clown's response includes sniggering reflections on sexual difference, suggesting perhaps some visible markers in the devils' costumes. Though their appearance is brief, it can be startling and entertaining, adding to the variety of supernatural thrills *Doctor Faustus* gives its audience. The earthy humor of the scene persists in the catalog of animals into which the Clown might be turned, and especially in his final choice of a flea. Fleas were associated in medieval poetry with a prurient and surreptitious sexuality, allegedly deriving from Ovid and surfacing later in Donne (Pride refers to 'Ovid's flea' in 2.3). With his jokes about tickling 'the pretty wenches' plackets,' the Clown invokes this tradition, and maintains the coarse, jocular tone with which the comic scenes ballast the play's grander aspects. This is one of the few scenes that is substantially longer in the A-text; the flea jokes are part of the extra comedy that fills out this version. At the close of the scene, Wagner seems to have successfully cowed the Clown into serving him, though we never again see them together. At the Clown's next appearance (if he is indeed Robin), he has become the one showing off his magic and lording it over his fellow.

Act II

Act II, scene i

One of the central moments in *Doctor Faustus* is that in which Faustus signs in blood his pact with the Devil. Exactly how this episode fits into the play's design, however, is not entirely clear. In the A-text, this scene is continuous with the episode in which Faustus tries to repent and Mephistopheles distracts him with the Seven Deadly Sins. The B-text separates those scenes with a brief chorus, spoken by Wagner, which appears before 3.1 in the A-text. Many modern editions, following the editorial practice of Bevington and Rasmussen, separate the two long Faustus/Mephistopheles scenes with a comic Robin/ Rafe episode that occurs later in both of the earliest editions. Because this reordering has become widely accepted, this text will follow that sequence and treat the signing of the pact as an independent, self-contained scene, 2.1. Regardless of sequence, the moment at which Faustus writes the deed in his own blood makes harrowing theatre, marking the point at which he, at least, believes he can no longer turn back from his bargain with Lucifer.

1–14 Faustus appears again in his study, probably revealed by the drawing of a curtain across the discovery space. The scene will require a table with pen, knife, paper, etc. This may remain in the discovery space or be pushed out onto the stage – important action needs to take place around it – or in a modern staging it may already be in the stage space somewhere. The scene takes place at midnight (see 1.3.101); if this is indicated in any way (by lighting, a striking clock, etc.), it might foreshadow the scene of Faustus's final hour in Act 5. Faustus may be informally dressed, alone in his study at midnight; at any rate, he will need to access his bare arm for the critical action that follows.

After the clowning of 1.4, Faustus's opening lines are stark and shocking, plunging the play back into the tragedy of Faustus's soul. The speech swings back and forth between the notions of damnation and salvation, repentance and despair. In the first six lines, Faustus commits himself fervently to the path he has chosen; his short statements, with their insistent negatives, suggest that he is trying to persuade himself to 'be resolute' in his course. He acknowledges his wavering in line 7, and momentarily thinks of turning to God. Thoughts of God dominate the speech – Faustus uses the word six times in the A-text speech, after only having referred to 'Jehovah' and 'Jove' previously. But most of Faustus's energy is devoted to reinforcing his pact with Beelzebub, which leads him to the particularly lurid and ghastly image of line 14.

15–21 Faustus's inner struggle becomes externalized with the appearance of the Good and Evil Angels, again invoking the *psychomachia* tradition from medieval drama. It is likely that they flank Faustus on either side of the stage, or perhaps appear above him in the playhouse gallery. The angels' nearly symmetrical admonitions continue the questions that persist throughout the play: can Faustus repent and save his soul? What stops him from doing so? Elizabethan spectators, invested in the religious struggles that had gripped their nation for 60 years, would have found these arguments compelling and even dangerous to hear.

22–37 In dismissing the Good Angel's promptings and calling on Mephistopheles, Faustus manifests the dependence he will increasingly come to have on his demonic companion: he uses the name four times in an eight-line speech. Faustus's appeal for 'good tidings' from Mephistopheles might be a blasphemous echo of the Angel's announcement of Christ's birth in Luke 2:10, according to Bevington and Rasmussen. Mephistopheles's various entrances afford interpretive scope; does he merely walk through a stage door in his friar's robe, or is there something supernatural or surprising about his appearance? Mephistopheles's request for a 'deed of gift' in Faustus's blood corresponds to medieval beliefs about diabolical practices, and adds both a commercial and a corporeal dimension to Faustus's bargain.

38–52 Faustus's questioning of Mephistopheles again recalls the Christian catechism. The replies are brief and matter-of-fact. The Latin proverb stating that 'misery loves company' might not be understood by many audience members, but some might get the general sense from the cognates '*miseris*' and '*socios,*' as well as Mephistopheles's shrugging demeanor. Modern productions some-times translate Mephistopheles's reply into English.

53–73 Faustus does indeed seem to 'stab [his] arm courageously,' as Mephistopheles requests, and the audience is treated to some form of theatrical trick whereby blood seems to come from the wound and run down his arm (it may be applied through a tube in the knife blade or some such device, but its visible presence seems important for the scene). Even more striking is the moment when Faustus's blood congeals and prevents his writing the deed. Mephistopheles's exit to 'fetch thee fire to dissolve it straight' is disturbingly immediate, giving the impression that he has often overcome this impediment. The moment affords Faustus a last brief, suspenseful soliloquy before signing the deed. He may address the theatre audience directly. His speech is charged with anxiety, asking five terse questions and twice repeating the phrase about giving away his soul. Mephistopheles returns with a chafer; presumably Faustus sets the congealed blood, held in a dish or vessel of some kind, on the hot coals. Some produc-tions have the fire applied to Faustus's arm directly, making even more apparent its connection to the fires of hell. Mephistopheles's gloating asides, here and at line 82, establish complicity with the audience and expose Faustus's vulnerability. The actor of Mephistopheles will need to consider how these lines square with the demon's apparent sympathy for Faustus in their first encounter.

74–85 Faustus's '*Consummatum est*' is one of many ironic, even blas-phemous appropriations of scripture. In signing his soul to the devil, Faustus speaks the Latin version of Christ's last words from the cross, 'It is finished' (John 19:30). Immediately thereafter, Faustus sees the words '*homo fuge*' written on his arm: another Biblical quotation from the admonition, in Timothy 6:11, to the man of God to fly worldly temptations. If the words are visible to the audience, they have presumably been inscribed before the play and then revealed when Faustus pushes up his sleeve. Mephistopheles distracts Faustus with another moment of supernatural theatricality, as at least two devils enter in rich apparel and dance. This 'show,' intended to 'delight' Faustus as well as the audience, reinforces an ongoing, perhaps ironic parallel between diablerie and the theatre itself.

86–118   The actual words of the contract are read out by Faustus from a property scroll (probably written in advance – it would take over 2 minutes to write out the whole of Faustus's deed). The contract is slightly altered from the version in the *Faust Book* source, and adds the detail about Faustus becoming a spirit. This provision might bear on the question of whether Faustus is eligible for salvation after signing the deed; the Evil Angel later comments on Faustus being a spirit and inaccessible to God's pity (2.3.13). This makes an interesting theological point, but for the purposes of theatrical suspense, the audience should probably feel there is at least the possibility of Faustus's repenting. The reading of the deed can be an occasion for tension, or perhaps humor. Faustus might rattle off the words lightly, as one would the fine print of a contract, or he might dwell over articles that give him pause. Lucifer's title, 'Prince of the East,' might raise a *frisson* of alarm, at least from the audience. The final provision of lines 110–11, about the devils carrying Faustus body and soul 'into their habitation wheresoever,' can be terrifying, or perhaps comic, in its use of legalistic euphemism: Faustus has chosen not to write or say 'hell.' The handing over of the deed can also be a charged theatrical moment – how reluctant or nonchalant is Faustus? His words at line 116 suggest a degree of frustration and bitterness, though they may also be played as a joke. How, in turn, does Mephistopheles receive the contract, and what does he do with it once he has it? The contract is an essential property, and the actors will give it an appropriate degree of importance in these moments.

119–29   Faustus's first action, once the contract is complete, is to inquire about hell – perhaps a clue to his psychological state, to an obsessive interest in the damnation in which he can't quite believe. Mephistopheles's first reply, 'Under the heavens,' can come across as facetious, and even raise an audience laugh. The fuller discussion of lines 122–9 may be delivered with cosmographical coolness or metaphysical anguish, but it has a gravity recalling Mephistopheles's previous speech at 1.3.78. The present speech has a certain rhetorical elegance, especially in the almost circular formulation of lines 125–6, and with the anaphoric repetition of 'And' at the beginning of lines. But the word the speech returns to insistently is 'hell,' and the chief point the speech makes is about hell's limitlessness in space and time. Mephistopheles may use the speech to tease or torment Faustus, or he may be blandly informative; but he will likely communicate something of his own experience of hell.

130–43   Faustus's response is flippant and dismissive. It has a bit of the tone of Marlowe's own alleged remarks to the effect that 'the first beginning of religion was only to keep men in awe' (part of the so-called Baines Note, a series of accusations leveled at Marlowe by an informant shortly before Marlowe's death). Whether Faustus (or indeed Marlowe) really believes 'hell's a fable' or is trying to convince himself, is for the actor to decide. Mephistopheles certainly gains the theatrical upper hand with his dry riposte (l. 131); the audience can be in little doubt that experience will indeed change Faustus's mind before the play is over. The line may raise a laugh, as may Mephistopheles's subsequent lines wherein he brandishes the scroll (l. 133) and asserts his own presence in hell (ll. 139–40). Faustus's responses could come across as mere pigheadedness, self-deceiving denial, or a kind of intellectual courage. In his embrace of what he believes to be the conditions of hell ('walking, disputing, etc.') he echoes his earlier association of himself with 'the old philosophers' (1.3.62). Faustus seems to imagine hell as something like Dante's limbo, a kind of ongoing philosophical seminar; in performance it is up to Mephistopheles to communicate that his experience is very different.

144–61   Faustus's sensual nature briefly reasserts itself in his somewhat sudden and unexpected request for a wife, an episode taken from the *Faust Book*. Mephistopheles abruptly rejects the request, at first giving no reason. Interestingly, Marlowe avoids the theological explicitness of the source, in which the Devil explains, 'wedlock is a chief institution ordained of God, and that hast thou promised to defy.'

The scene provides an opportunity for both comedy and spectacle with the appearance of the devil-bride. Mephistopheles exits and brings her in, perhaps somehow parodying the ritual of a wedding ceremony. The A-text stage direction specifies both female attire and fireworks, which may have been tossed about the stage or actually fired from the devil-bride's costume. In their scholarly edition of *Doctor Faustus*, Bevington and Rasmussen cite a demon in the medieval play *The Castle of Perseverance* who has fireworks 'in his hands and in his ears and in his arse' (1993, 145). Marlowe's demon, as a 'hot whore,' may have used something similarly crude and explicit; at the Globe in 2012, the devil-bride had fireworks shooting from her breasts and between her legs.

The devil-bride is one of the play's many brief moments of startling supernatural showmanship; she appears in both versions of the play, though only the A-text specifies fireworks. Following her exit, Mephistopheles's words take on a seductive and erotic tone at lines 156–61, recalling Marlowe's Ovidian love poetry – though the comparison of the prospective Courtesan's beauty with 'bright Lucifer before his fall' could have a chilling effect. At any rate, Faustus says nothing further on the subject, and his sexual desires, which generate a good deal of action in the *Faust Book*, are not mentioned again in Marlowe's play until the scene with Helen of Troy.

162–80 As Faustus says nothing, Mephistopheles diverts his attention to the powers he will wield, producing a book of magic, another important prop. The appearance of the book could be an occasion for stage trickery or sleight of hand, or Mephistopheles may just pull it from under his robes. Faustus may or may not be impressed – his 'Thanks, Mephistopheles' could sound comically understated to a modern audience (l. 169). In a prose conversation in the A-text only, Faustus asks for further knowledge – of spells, cosmography, and plants – and Mephistopheles '*turn[s] to them*' in the book he has already given. There could be a note of humorous anti-climax in the exchange, contrasting the grandeur of Faustus's requests with the flat matter-of-factness of Mephistopheles's responses: 'Here they are too.'

181–2 The end of this scene, if it is the end, is rather abrupt and bathetic, given the magnitude of what has gone before. The scene order in the A-text, which runs this scene directly into 2.3, is not impossible, though it requires Faustus having a very sudden and unexplained change of heart. It is likely that some scenes are missing or out of order in both the A- and B-texts, and some sort of editorial intervention is necessary.

Faustus's evident frustration at line 181 may suggest an awakening to the shortcomings of his bargain; he has sold his soul for knowledge that can be contained in a single book. Mephistopheles's blasé reassurance ('Tut, I warrant thee') completes the deflating effect. An alternative reading of Faustus's 'O, thou art deceived' might be as an aside to himself, a recognition that he has been ensnared by the Devil; this seems less likely but might make a stronger dramatic choice.

The B-text ends the scene on a more positive and conclusive note, with Faustus promising to keep the 'sweet book … as chary as [his] life.'

Act II, scene ii

If Bevington and Rasmussen are correct, and this first Robin/Rafe scene follows 2.1, then the business of the conjuring book might link the two scenes together. Robin could even be seen stealing the book – either the one Mephistopheles just gave Faustus or another from Faustus's study. This brief scene extends the notion of a debased apostolic succession of conjurors, if Robin was the Clown in 1.4. Faustus's magic first trickled down to Wagner, then went in turn to Robin, who is now showing it off to Rafe. Just as Faustus's magic powers become corrupted in his own use of them, so the magic employed by other characters quickly reaches the lowest common denominator of human appetite.

1–6 Whether he was the Clown in 1.4 or not, Robin is plainly identifiable as a low comic character from his stable-boy's clothing and exuberant prose address to the audience. His immediate preoccupation with sex further establishes the coarse humor of the scene, with a winking pun on 'circles' (l. 3) and the more explicit desires of lines 4–5. The close of the speech might indicate a recognition that Rafe is not yet quite the Lothario he intends to be.

7–19 Robin enters to call Rafe back to work, but Rafe quickly reverses their statuses by playing up the importance and danger of his conjuring. Presumably they are at about the same lowly rank, though Robin tends to have the upper hand in their interactions through his blustering self-confidence. The innuendos of the scene continue in almost every line, from the rubbing and chafing of 8–9 to the blowing-up and dismembering of 12–13; how heavily the actors want to hit these will vary by production, but some amount of leering and gesturing is likely to accompany these lines. Lines 18–19 show Robin's explicit desire to cuckold his master, with jokes on 'forehead', 'private', and 'bear.'

20–36 When Robin reveals the powers of his book, it is significant that the first use he mentions for it is to access limitless supplies of liquor. The lowly appetites of the two ostlers foreshadow the debasement of Faustus's own magic; though whereas he conjures Helen of Troy, they are content with Nan Spit, the kitchen maid. Her name, appropriate to her employment as a cook's drudge or turnspit, also allows Robin and Rafe some luridly explicit reflections on the sexual conquest they hope to make of her. The earthy imagery is carried through to the horse-bread with which Rafe proposes to reward the Devil and the filthy boots which occupy the two stable hands on their exit.

In the B-text Rafe is called Dick, and the scene is ordered and worded differently. Nonetheless, it contains the same elements: the stolen conjuring book, the lecherousness and resentment embodied in the desire to cuckold the master, the fantasies about limitless drinking on the Devil's tab. Nan Spit gets no mention, and oddly it is Dick, rather than the parish maidens, who is expected to dance naked. The B-text does have one quality joke in which Robin laboriously tries to read out the magic spell letter by letter, but on the whole the scenes do the same work and there is not much to choose between them.

Act II, scene iii

This crucial, central scene is built with a dynamic that repeats often throughout the play. Faustus, despairing, considers repentance, and then is lured or bullied back into his path toward damnation. Here he is wooed with knowledge, threatened by Lucifer, and finally dazzled with the show of the Seven Deadly Sins, one of the play's signature *coups de théâtre*. This scene, placed just in the center of the A-text, marks the end of the initial action of Faustus selling his soul; the remainder will deal with his 24 years of adventures and his tragic final hour.

1–11 Faustus opens his speech of repentance with the language of the Psalms (8:1), perhaps looking up into the sky or at the 'heavens' that were painted on the roof of the Elizabethan stage (l. 1). Mephistopheles's reply uses the flattering language of Renaissance humanism, invoking the dignity of man and his central place in the universe (ll. 6–9). The rhetoric backfires, and in a strongly balanced and alliterative line, Faustus again resolves on repentance (l. 10).

12–18   The exchange with the Good and Evil Angels addresses the recurrent question of the state of Faustus's soul and the possibility of his repentance. The word 'buzzeth' stands out, giving a concrete sense of how the Angels might manifest themselves to Faustus (l. 14). Otherwise this exchange is stark in its insistent repetition of a small number of potent words: 'God' (4 times), 'pity' (4), 'repent' (4), 'spirit' (2).

19–37   Faustus's speech of despair and exalted hedonism is not technically a soliloquy, since Mephistopheles remains onstage, but it is likely treated as one, with Faustus addressing the audience directly as he reflects on his spiritual struggles and transcendent pleasures. The speech breaks into three parts. In the first (ll. 18–25), Faustus comments on the hardening of his heart (a phrase that recalls God's treatment of the Pharaoh in Exodus) and his consequent inability to repent. The lengthy list of weapons through which Faustus is tempted to suicide gives the actor a chance to build the intensity of Faustus's despair (years later, Shakespeare would duplicate this effect in *Othello* 3.3). The phrase 'long ere this' creates an odd sort of double time scheme for the play; this is ostensibly midnight of the day on which the play began, but this speech gives the effect of a much longer flow of action. For the middle part of the speech (ll. 26–32), Faustus muses on his pleasures in lines of typically Marlovian richness and soaring sensuality. This is a tone we will hear again in the paean to Helen of Troy, and it lifts the scene from despair for a few moments with elegant classical names, emotion-suffused themes, and lush diction ('ravishing', 'melodious'). There is a tone of romance, and perhaps homoeroticism, in the alliterative line 30, with its reference to 'my Mephistopheles.' Finally, in the last section, Faustus rejects repentance and questions Mephistopheles about astronomy, showing once more the thirst for knowledge that was one of his original motivations.

38–65   The astronomical question-and-answer session between Faustus and Mephistopheles, with its Latin phrases and technical terms, may go over the audience's heads. On the other hand, at least some Elizabethan spectators would have had a keen interest in debates about the nature of the physical universe. Copernicus's heliocentric model, though published in 1543, had not yet taken hold internationally, but the geocentric universe of Ptolemy had become increasingly problematic. Though the material discussed here is fairly basic – 'freshmen's suppositions,' as Faustus disparagingly calls it – it reflects some of the real questions astronomers were grappling with in explaining observations of planetary motion. Dramatically, the conversation develops the sense of Faustus's interest in extending the bounds of knowledge, and Mephistopheles's easy but limited willingness to provide certain kinds of information. The astronomy debate switches back and forth between verse and prose, with both speakers using some of each. They tend toward prose when the material is particularly technical, or the speaker's attitude is somewhat offhand or dismissive, as at lines 46–8 or 54–7.

66–74 An audience lulled into confusion or inattention by the cosmological technicalities of the preceding speeches will be brought up short by this exchange. After the polysyllabic Latinate diction of the previous conversation, the stark, simple phrasing of 'Tell me who made the world' has tremendous power. Mephistopheles's refusal is even starker. Immediately, the emotional temperature of the scene goes up, as a scientific discussion becomes a spiritual showdown. In one of the most intense exchanges between the two characters, Faustus and Mephistopheles probably face each other at close range, center stage. Faustus may wheedle or plead, using the phrase 'sweet Mephistopheles.' Mephistopheles, for the first time, shows real signs of anger ('Move me not'), and becomes threatening in a way he has not been since his initial appearance as a dragon in 1.3. His utterances become terse and imperative, and his sudden menacing exit at line 74 builds suspense and anxiety about what will ensue if Faustus provokes him further.

Most editors format the exchange as prose, but there are lines that scan as pentameters (e.g. Faustus's line 73, and the imperative from Mephistopheles that precedes it). Further, the basic iambic rhythm into which much of the exchange falls can create tension around some of the shorter lines, suggesting built-in pauses. In any event, it is a moment of intense drama that maintains the high stakes of Faustus's predicament.

75–83 Faustus's impulse toward repentance again prompts the appearance of the Good and Evil Angels, this time focused on the question of whether it is 'too late,' a phrase repeated three times. There is a critical difference between the A- and B-texts at line 79. The A-text reads 'Never too late, if Faustus can repent,' whereas the B-text reads 'if Faustus will repent' (l. 80). The latter reading is perhaps more hopeful, whereas the A-text seems to imply that the choice of repentance may not be in Faustus's power. There has been a lot of critical emphasis on a line that may pass quickly in the theatre; but the way this exchange is played may create a more or less ominous atmosphere. In any event, the moment when Faustus calls out to Christ and instead receives a visit from Lucifer is likely to make a powerful statement about the state of Faustus's soul and the possibility, or impossibility, of his redemption.

84–106 The sudden appearance of Lucifer, Beelzebub, and Mephistopheles offers yet another opportunity for supernatural spectacle. While Mephistopheles probably still has the innocuous appearance of a Franciscan friar, the other devils are under no such restraints, and theatre companies are likely to give their costume designers and makeup artists free rein for a terrifying presentation of these characters. Medieval representations of devils, both in the visual arts and in drama, often featured animalistic elements such as horns, wings, hooves, fangs, and tails; any or all of these might have adorned Lucifer and Beelzebub in an early modern production. Their entrance, like those of other devils, might have been accompanied by fireworks, together with thunder or other frightening sound effects. For an Elizabethan audience it would have been a frightening moment, but probably also a gratifying and exciting one; in a play on this subject, the appearance of devils was likely a high selling point. In the medieval play of *Mankind*, the vice characters demand money from the audience before they will bring on the principal devil; it is probable that the appearance of Lucifer in Faustus was similarly anticipated as a theatrical thrill.

For modern theatre-makers, whose audiences are generally more secular in orientation, such moments present both a challenge and an opportunity. While it may be difficult to instill the fear of real devils that supposedly affected Elizabethan spectators, such characters can still terrify. Films such as *Rosemary's Baby* (1968), *The Exorcist* (1973), and *The Omen* (1976) showed that twentieth-century viewers could still find the demonic truly disturbing, and they continue to spawn sequels and reboots to this day. The bestial iconography of medieval devils remains in the communal memory, and retains at least some of its power to shock. In the modern theatre, the resources of sound, lighting, movement, costume, and prosthetic makeup can give these kinds of appearances substantial theatrical impact, even for a largely secular audience.

Lucifer challenges Faustus directly, overhearing and responding to his previous words. His entrance may be immediate, or after a suspenseful pause. The fact that Lucifer appears when Faustus calls on Christ may suggest that Faustus is already beyond salvation; at any rate, it implies that heaven is much more remote from the world of the play than hell. Interestingly, Faustus assumes the situation is worse than it is, and that the devils have come to take him to hell immediately (l. 89); so that Lucifer's tone becomes just slightly reassuring in the succeeding lines. In the B-text, Beelzebub takes several of these lines, including the jocular reference to the Devil's dam and the promise of pastime; he never speaks in the A-text. The B-text arrangement allows for a sort of good cop/bad cop dynamic, with Lucifer as the more threatening and Beelzebub the more wheedling devil; but either version contains a mixture of menace and cajoling. Faustus's capitulation is immediate and immoderate; his promise to slay ministers and pull churches down may be comic in its exaggerated zeal (ll. 95–8). Lucifer's final line also can have a testy humor about it; Faustus has put his foot in his mouth by mentioning Adam and Creation, offending the Devil in his eagerness to placate him. The reference to the Seven Deadly Sins as a 'show' has a metatheatrical resonance, but also a quality of comic understatement (l. 105). Faustus sits to observe, probably in a chair from his desk; this is one of the only times when he is specifically required to leave the standing position. This moment of repose may be welcome for the actor, but it suggests a vulnerability or weakening on the part of Faustus.

107–9 In the A-text Lucifer simply calls offstage for the Sins to appear; in the B-text he exits to fetch them, presumably returning with them, though he does not speak for another 50 lines. Both texts have the stage direction, '*Enter the* SEVEN DEADLY SINS.' Allegorical personifications of Sins were common in medieval morality plays, and there may have been traditions in place for costuming, attributes, and behaviors. Edward Alleyn's company actually performed an Elizabethan play on the subject, though only an outline of the plot of one part survives. The words of the Sins themselves are perhaps the best guide to their representation onstage. Any production will devote a good deal of craft and ingenuity to the appearance of these alarming figures. Modern stage history has included puppets, decaying corpses, huge masks, and dance-like groupings that incorporated all seven performers into each individual Sin. In any event, the Sins represent a great theatrical opportunity, and the narrative is suspended for some minutes for their 'show.'

110–17 The play follows more or less the same pattern with each Sin, with Faustus very briefly asking each to identify itself, and the Sin replying with reference to its parentage, nature, and inclinations. The Sins are ordered according to a traditional grouping of sins of the spirit and sins of the flesh. Pride, by tradition the original deadly sin through the association with Lucifer's fall, is an appropriate figure to go first. He may well assert his precedence over his fellows in some aggressive or haughty manner. While his disdain for parentage and his contempt for his surroundings fit with medieval notions of the sin, more than half of what Pride has to say relates to the prurient sexuality of 'Ovid's flea,' recalling the Clown's wish in 1.4.

118–23 Covetousness's references to 'an old leathern bag' and 'my good chest' may give a clue to his appearance or properties.

124–30 Wrath comes third in the A-text, fourth, after Envy, in the B-text. Medieval sources had varying orders for the seven deadly sins, though many, like Marlowe's, kept the sins of the mind separate from those of the body. Wrath's reference to 'this case of rapiers' suggests that he, like Covetousness, is identified by a particular property or visual attribute.

131–8 Envy's attribute is leanness; presumably he was played by a very thin actor in threadbare clothes. He would likely have worn the green or yellow color associated with this emotion since medieval times. His challenge at line 137 is presumably directed at Faustus, who has been invited to sit earlier; but it could just as easily be given to audience members seated in the galleries above the stage; his cry of 'Come down!' may support this reading.

139–53 Gluttony is the most loquacious sin in both A- and B-texts, referring to grandparents and godparents as well as his parents. His heavy alliteration on 'm,' 'p,' 'g,' and 'b' fits with a jowly sluggishness of speech. He is likely plodding in movement and padded in costume; perhaps he eats and drinks during the scene. Faustus interacts with him more than with the others, displaying increasing confidence, hostility, or amusement as the 'show' goes on.

154–9 Appropriately, Sloth speaks the fewest words of the sins in the B-text, and his speech is twice interrupted by yawns indicated by 'Heigh-ho!' In the A-text his request to be carried by Gluttony and Lechery is probably refused, but he may require some sort of transport on and off stage; he speaks of being 'brought' and 'carried.'

160–3 Lechery is the only one of the sins for whom a gender is specified ('Mistress Minx'). The extra 'I, Sir?' in B may indicate an actor's embellishment of teasing interaction with Faustus; some level of physical provocation seems likely, such as her sitting on Faustus's lap. On Marlowe's stage Lechery would have been a boy actor in seductive female dress. In modern adaptations this character has taken a number of grotesque or alluring forms, from the skeletal temptress played by Sara Kestleman in the 1968 RSC production to Raquel Welch's Lillian Lust in the Peter Cook/Dudley Moore film *Bedazzled*. Along with the encounters with the devil-bride and Helen of Troy, the moment with Lechery is one of few points where Faustus's sexual appetite, a major feature of the *Faust Book*, is put in the foreground.

164–77 The exit of the Sins is accompanied, in the B-text, by a piper – possibly one of the Sins themselves – who leads them at Lucifer's command. If this is a musical moment, it is one of few specifically called for. Faustus's response to the Sins seems mainly to be one of spectatorial pleasure; 'This feeds my soul' marks an irony that may be chilling or comical (especially if Faustus has been visibly aroused by Lechery's blandishments). If the Sins are represented as grotesque or repellent, Faustus's delight in them can be an index of his moral blindness. Lucifer produces yet another book for Faustus – books are the chief props – perhaps employing some supernatural sleight of hand. Faustus's effusive thanks provide another moment of irony, as he exits eagerly with Mephistopheles.

Act III, Chorus

The speech that introduces Act III (if it is correctly labeled as such) is spoken in the A-text by Wagner, in the B-text by the anonymous Chorus who introduced the play. Wagner seems an unlikely speaker in some ways, since the passage relates Faustus's cosmological adventures in a dragon-drawn chariot, as well as his arrival at Rome, to which Wagner could hardly be privy. If Wagner does give the speech, he may inject a note of weary sarcasm into some of the loftier rhetoric, and his 'As I guess' at line 8 may have an edge of doubt or mockery. Taken at face value, the speech is exalted in tone, repeatedly using the imagery of height, and echoing both Christian and classical sources in its elevated language ('Graven,' 'Jove,' 'firmament,' 'Olympus,' 'chariot'). While the Wagner-chorus in A quickly moves on to locate Faustus in Rome, taking up only 11 lines in total, the B-chorus goes on for a full 25 lines, with much more detail about 'the tropics, zones, and quarters of the sky.' Whether written by Marlowe or not, the B-speech does echo the language of the *Faust Book*, and goes along with the general tenor of linguistic extravagance associated with Faustus's zodiacal adventures in both playtexts as well as the source. This longer B-chorus also includes the rather inconsequential detail of Faustus's temporary return home from his travels; in A this return is mentioned in the chorus that follows this scene. Both choruses end by setting the scene in Rome, and here the high language is clearly intended as ironic, given the anti-Catholic satire that ensues in the episode of 'Holy Peter's feast.'

Act III, scene i

The scene with the Pope is primarily comic in both versions. In Marlowe's England, anti-Catholic burlesques of the clergy were by no means uncommon, and other playwrights had put the Pope onstage in similarly irreverent ways. John Bale's 1538 *King Johan*, a Henrician combination of chronicle and morality play, brings the Pope onstage in the character of 'Usurped Power.' Marlowe himself shows an anti-Catholic bent in several plays, with Christian hypocrites in *Tamburlaine*, venial Friars in *The Jew of Malta*, and the diabolical Duke of Guise in *The Massacre at Paris*. Anti-Catholic feeling was high enough that Faustus and Mephistopheles become, effectively, the heroes of the episode, playing practical jokes that mock clerical pretension and temporarily make the audience (and Faustus, perhaps) forget the grave situation of Faustus's soul. The episode with the Pope thus introduces the central phase of the play in which Faustus becomes a trickster-hero performing entertaining feats with the help of his sidekick Mephistopheles. In the A-text the episode in Rome is self-contained and entirely comic; in the B-text it takes on a more serious political dimension, and is linked with the subsequent episodes in the court of the Emperor.

1–19 Both texts begin with an extensive travelogue in which Faustus and Mephistopheles recount some of their peregrinations, in passages based closely on *The English Faust Book*. Faustus's first speech, in appreciative and stately verse with a hint of travel-brochure hyperbole, invokes the 'airy mountain tops' surrounding Trier and the 'grove of fruitful vines' that line the Rhine Valley. Faustus notes the precise urban planning of Naples, and recounts the medieval legend that Virgil magically tunneled through the hill of Posillipo – perhaps reflecting admiringly on the work of one he considers a fellow necromantic artist. Faustus's enthusiasm for the 'sumptuous temple' in Venice, though it mistakenly grants St Mark's a star-threatening 'aspiring top,' conveys the Marlovian regard for opulent splendor, especially in the B-text, where it is 'roofed aloft with curious work in gold' (B. 20).

20–49 This whole sequence functions almost cinematically, moving from the extreme wide shot of Faustus's dragon-borne space-flight in the choral speech, through Faustus's more topographical but still airborne account of the great cities of Europe, then narrowing down to Mephistopheles's evocation of the highlights of Rome, and finally zooming in to the Pope's chamber in the Vatican. Mephistopheles mentions sights that remain tourist destinations today – the hills, bridges, and antiquities of Rome, including Castel Sant'Angelo and the Egyptian obelisk that stands before St Peter's. The original production perhaps added a visual dimension to Mephistopheles's description. Among the props inventoried in Henslowe's Diary is something listed as the 'city of Rome,' perhaps a backcloth or physical structure, which may have been revealed at this point. The numerological details of Mephistopheles's account – seven hills, four bridges, double cannons matching the number of days in the year – both add to Rome's grandeur and subtly recall the numbered days of Faustus's 'years of liberty', mentioned at line 61 of the B-text. Another touch of ironic foreshadowing comes as Faustus, in his enthusiasm for seeing the sights of Rome, swears by the kingdoms and rivers of hell.

50–9   The suggestion that Faustus meddle in 'Holy Peter's feast' comes from Mephistopheles, but in the generally anti-Catholic world of the play it can probably have no particular role in the plot to secure Faustus's damnation. The jocular references to 'bald-pate friars,' 'belly-cheer,' 'folly,' 'sport,' and 'merriment' set the tone for the scene to follow. When Faustus asks to be an actor in the spectacle, Mephistopheles presumably attires him in another item from Henslowe's inventory, a 'robe for to go invisible.' At the equivalent point in the B-text Mephistopheles gives Faustus a 'girdle' and charms him with a magic wand to make him 'invisible to all are here' (B. 3.2.18).

60 s.d.   The stage directions for the Pope's entry differ in the two texts, and mark serious divergences in the scenes that follow. The A-text calls for the Pope and the Cardinal of Lorraine, attended by friars, to enter 'to the banquet,' suggesting perhaps that a table has been set from the beginning of the scene; the comic hijinks begin almost immediately at their entrance. The B-text here inserts an entire scene invoking the twelfth-century conflict between the Popes and the Emperor Frederick I, which eventuated in a rival pope being established and then suppressed. Conflating a number of different figures and events taken from Foxe's *Book of Martyrs*, the author of the B-text introduces Pope Adrian and the antipope, Bruno, who is 'led in chains' and cast down at the Pope's feet as his 'footstool.' This highly dramatic action, whether written by Marlowe or (more likely) not, is characteristic of him; it recalls 4.2 of *Tamburlaine Part I*, in which Tamburlaine abuses the conquered Bajazeth in a similar manner. The first line of that scene, 'Bring out my footstool,' is closely echoed by the Pope's first line, 'Cast down our footstool,' and the scenes proceed in similar acts of protest and subjugation. In asserting his power over Bruno, Pope Adrian invokes the power of excommunication (employed in 1570 against Queen Elizabeth), and the doctrine of papal infallibility, both of which would have provoked strongly negative reactions from an English Protestant audience. Pope Adrian's arrogance in treading upon Bruno's body, and his haughty threats to 'smite with death' the Church's enemies, make him a more powerful and sinister figure than the merely comic Pope of the A-text.

The fact that the B-text antipope's name is Bruno (changed from the historical Victor) may have had some resonance in early performances. Bruno is threatened with being burned at the stake as a heretic, just as Giordano Bruno was burned in Rome by the Inquisition in 1600. The historical Bruno, a heretical friar, scientist, and alleged magician, had traveled to England in the 1580s and taught briefly at Wittenberg. His story has some interesting points of connection with *Doctor Faustus*, though of course Marlowe can have known nothing of his death, having died himself 7 years before. Whoever introduced Bruno to the B-text, it is just possible they may have had the historical Bruno partly in mind. At any rate, the name Bruno might have called up this association for some Elizabethan audience members, especially after 1600.

In the B-text Faustus and Mephistopheles intervene on Bruno's behalf by disguising themselves as friars and then aiding in Bruno's escape. They also steal the Pope's triple crown, causing two cardinals to take the blame for its loss (a 'Pope's mitre' is listed in Henslowe's inventory of the company's props). These events augment the anti-Catholicism of the whole episode, and heighten the sense of Faustus and Mephistopheles as playful co-conspirators.

60–80   In both texts, the chief comic action of the Rome episode is the disruption of the Pope's dinner, carried out by the invisible Faustus and Mephistopheles. There is probably a table onstage (in the B-text the Pope invites the cardinals to sit), and the scene may arouse blasphemous visual associations with Jesus' Last Supper. Both texts follow the same series of disruptions: Faustus startles the Pope by speaking while invisible, he snatches away the Pope's food, steals or spills his wine, and strikes him for crossing himself. The coarse business with food and drink and the exaggerated reactions of the terrified clerics to their unseen tormentors can make this a very funny scene. The audience's complicit knowledge – unlike the other characters, we can see Faustus and Mephistopheles, and so anticipate with pleasure their acts of mockery – ensures a supportive response to the crude slapstick. The scene contains further anti-Catholic satire, as one of the clerics suggests the invisible troublemaker may be a ghost from Purgatory seeking a pardon (Protestants denied the existence of Purgatory and derided the granting of postmortem indulgences). In the B-text, the Pope specifically attacks the offending spirits as 'Lollards'; Lollardry was an English religious movement whose criticism of the Church anticipated the Protestant Reformation.

81–100 The scene ends with a brief coda in which the friars re-enter to sing a dirge. This remains in the comic vein – the contrast between the friars' somber plainchant and the indignities it recounts is irresistibly humorous – though the references to excommunication might strike a slightly more serious note. While 'Bell, book and candle' was common sarcastic shorthand for excommunication (Shakespeare uses it similarly in *King John*), Faustus's playfully dwelling on and inverting the phrase might remind us of his own state of jeopardy. His laughing reference to an action intended 'to curse Faustus to hell' might suddenly seem foolishly cavalier – Faustus will indeed be cursed to hell by the end of the play.

The friars' line 'Cursed be he that disturbeth our holy dirge' suggests that Faustus and Mephistopheles continue their mischief throughout, perhaps striking the friars, spilling wine, or moving objects about in frightening ways. As the scene ends, they *'beat the Friars, and fling fireworks among them, and so exeunt.'* This explosive finale, one of several uses of pyrotechnics, rounds out one of the loudest and busiest scenes of the central sequence of Faustus's adventures.

Act III, scene ii

Before Faustus's next appearance, in the court of the Emperor, both the A- and B- texts include a comic interlude with the clown Robin and his companion, Rafe or Dick. Assuming that their first scene occurs earlier (many editors, following Bevington and Rasmussen, place it after 2.1), the present episode involves their stealing a goblet from the Vintner of an inn. This incident provides some quality slapstick, and introduces Mephistopheles briefly to the comic underplot. The farcical business with the goblet recalls the antics of Faustus in stealing the Pope's wine, equating Faustus's pranks with tavern horseplay.

1–4 Robin's opening lines remind the audience of the magic book he has stolen, which he displays with a portentous Latin tag. His lowly aspiration for his new power – as an ostler, his immediate concern is for what his horses shall eat – parallels Faustus's frivolities in the main plot. Indeed, Robin's line 'as long as this lasts' suggests that he has a somewhat more pragmatic attitude than Faustus. Proud of the elevated status he believes magic will give him, Robin condescends to the Vintner as a 'Drawer' or tapster.

5–24 The Vintner enters seeking his goblet. Robin bluffs with denial and abuse: his 'you are but a *etc.*' may indicate an unprintable insult, an opportunity for improvisation, or a smirking euphemism. The clowns pass the goblet back and forth as the Vintner searches them by turns. Both the sleight of hand with the goblet and the business of searching afford rich comic opportunities. Are the clowns ticklish, indignant, or perhaps sexually self-conscious as the Vintner pats them down? Is the goblet hidden in clothes or hats, tossed through the air, even temporarily passed off to an audience member? At some point, the Vintner must be on the point of discovering it, and Robin decides to raise the stakes by employing his new conjuring skills.

25–37 Surprisingly, the conjuration is successful. Just as he did for Faustus in 1.3, Mephistopheles appears at the sound of his name. His appearance here may slightly contradict his earlier assertion to Faustus that he can't be involuntarily drawn by magic spells; the comedy of this moment lies in his exasperation that he has been brought all the way from Constantinople by the two clowns. The arrival of Mephistopheles turns the scene to verse. His presence brings the high and low plots together for the first time, and the discordant conjunction is richly comic. Robin's cringing offer of an alehouse supper to make up for Mephistopheles's long journey evokes both sympathy and laughter.

38–44 The end of this scene provides a good example of the multiplicity and instability of the play we know as *Doctor Faustus*. There seem to be at least three different versions of the final interaction of Mephistopheles and the clowns, maybe more, inscribed across the surviving texts. The A-text combines two different possibilities for the end of the scene, as Mephistopheles enters twice and twice transforms the miscreants into animals (including, in the first version, the hapless Vintner). The B-text has yet another version. In A, pyrotechnics are once again employed to heighten the diabolical comedy; on Mephistopheles's first entrance, he '*sets squibs at their backs*' and '*they run about.*' There is confusion in the various versions about who becomes which animal – the options include an ass and a bear – but one of the principal clowns is probably turned to an ape and one to a dog. They may simply adopt the physical movements of the animals, or there may be some deft adoption of masks or other costume pieces; Henslowe included '1 black dog' among the company's inventory of properties. At any rate, part of the comedy is that the intended punishment is not necessarily taken as such by the two clowns. They are so bestial themselves that they can see advantages in their new subhuman forms.

Act IV, Chorus

This speech, found only in the A-text and probably out of place there after 3.1, raises the same questions as the other Faustus choruses. Who is the speaker – an anonymous presenter figure, Wagner, or perhaps some other character from the play? What is the speaker's attitude toward Faustus's actions? The overall tone seems celebratory, with many words conveying a positive spirit of Renaissance achievement: 'rarest,' 'learned,' 'admired,' 'wondered,' 'fame.' Lines 4–5 allow for a more personal tone toward Faustus on the part of the speaker, whether of sincere affection or, perhaps, of irony and disdain. If the speaker is Wagner, for instance, he might here be sarcastic or effusive; his other appearances establish a capacity for insolence but also for loyalty to Faustus.

Some of the action described by the Chorus might be enacted in dumbshow: Faustus's return to his friends, his disquisitions on astrology, and his general adulation could be performed as part of a transition to the upcoming scene. The smooth, regular, end-stopped lines of the speech, layered into lengthy sentences, give a kind of grandiosity to this passage, setting up Faustus as a European celebrity feted by kings. The fittingly pompous appellation 'Carolus the Fifth' introduces the Emperor, whose court may be assembling on the stage as the speech concludes. The staging suggests a throne for the Emperor, and there are likely to be supernumerary courtiers, banners, trumpets, and so forth to add to the splendor of the scene. In the B-text Bruno, the Saxon antipope, is also present, having been rescued from Rome and brought to Germany by a spirit in the aftermath of 3.1.

Act IV, scene i

The episode of Faustus before the Emperor presents the greatest single divergence between the A- and B-texts. In both versions, Faustus conjures Alexander and his paramour at the Emperor's request, and magically places a pair of horns on the head of a skeptical Knight. The B-text passage, however, adds other characters and goes on for several scenes, comprising around a fifth of the entire play. In either case, the episode continues the representation, derived from the *Faust Book*, of Faustus's growing fame and prankish adventures, mostly forestalling any sense of the reckoning to come.

1–11 The A-text Emperor, perhaps surprisingly, begins in prose, though his speech is somewhat formal. His reference to a familiar spirit suggests that Mephistopheles is not visible to the characters other than Faustus, or indeed, that he may not yet be present in the scene: he is not mentioned in the entry direction. The Emperor comes quickly to the point: he wishes a demonstration of Faustus's magic. His reassurances at the end of the speech are a reminder that magic was considered witchcraft, and might imperil the user.

12–18 The Knight's sneering aside briefly punctures the formality of the scene. Faustus responds to the Emperor with courtly prose, tempering obsequious deference with urbane self-confidence.

19–30 The first part of the Emperor's speech is printed as prose in the A-text, but it has a stately iambic rhythm and many editors have recast it as verse. The Emperor's solitary reflections on the feats of his predecessors continue the theme of earthly fame introduced in the chorus speech.

31–67 The Emperor's request to see Alexander the Great, like the later desire of the Scholars and Faustus to see Helen of Troy, is borrowed from the *Faust Book*, but it resonates with the enthusiasm for classical antiquity and exotic grandeur that is a hallmark of Marlowe's poetry and drama. The fact that Alexander and his paramour will be merely phantoms, their real bodies having been 'consumed to dust,' highlights the theme of illusory glory (cf. Hamlet's graveside meditation on 'the noble dust of Alexander'). The Knight continues his suspicious asides. At line 58 he first challenges Faustus directly, perhaps in a different part of the stage; the Emperor does not acknowledge their quarrel. (In the B-text the equivalent character, named Benvolio, makes his derisive asides from a window above the stage, as in the *Faust Book*.) The reference to Actaeon sets up Faustus's revenge, for which he elicits Mephistopheles's help, perhaps with a wink or gesture. (Actaeon was a hunter who saw Diana bathing; she turned him into a stag and he was killed by his own hounds.)

68–73   The appearance of Alexander and his paramour is another of the play's signature moments of supernatural showmanship. There is probably stately music, and the characters are in exotic period costumes: the Emperor has specifically requested that they be in 'their right shapes, gesture and attire/ They used to wear during their time of life' (39–40). Modern productions will probably employ special lighting, makeup, and movement to help create the sense of ghostly images of long-dead heroes. The B-text presentation of this moment is much more elaborate, and calls for an eventful dumbshow in which Alexander kills the Persian king, Darius, and presents his crown to his paramour. It also adds a further moment of drama in which the Emperor, though warned not to speak to the spirits, *'offers to embrace them, which Faustus seeing suddenly stays him'* (B. 4.1.102.4–5 s.d.) The magical atmosphere of the phantoms' appearance is slightly broken by the Emperor's curiosity about the 'wart or mole' on the lady's neck; this homely detail adds a touch of comedy.

74–99   After the spirits' exit, Faustus enjoys his revenge over the skeptical Knight. The horns he wears, which have been affixed to his head backstage, make him the butt of the usual Elizabethan jokes about cuckoldry. In the B-text Faustus pursues his revenge further, again alluding to the story of Actaeon and calling up a trio of demonic hounds to threaten Benvolio with their 'bloody fangs.' They may actually appear onstage, or at any rate Benvolio seems to feel their torments at line 153. In both texts Faustus is persuaded by the Emperor to relent, and the horns are removed. Faustus jocularly warns his enemy to 'speak well of scholars' hereafter. In the A-text, the Knight leaves without protest, and is never heard from again. In the B-text, however, Benvolio refuses to heed Faustus's warning, leading to two more scenes of attempted revenge and supernatural comeuppance.

B-text Act IV, scene ii and Act IV, scene iii

These B-text Benvolio scenes are notable for two reasons, which may be suggestive about the way *Doctor Faustus* was received in the Elizabethan theatre. First of all, the scenes contain more of the stage trickery and comic magic that has been featured in the Pope and Emperor episodes. Second, as in those scenes, Faustus is more or less unequivocally the comic hero, besting his proud adversaries and presumably gaining the enthusiastic support of the audience. There is almost no mention of Faustus's bargain or the jeopardy of his soul, and Mephistopheles plays only a minimal role as an agent of Faustus's revenge on Benvolio. If these scenes are part of the 'additions' for which Henslowe paid in 1602, it seems he wanted to give his audiences more high-spirited magical entertainment – suggesting that this is what they responded to most.

Benvolio and his companions Frederick and Martino set up two separate ambushes for Faustus. The scene is specifically defined as a 'grove' (l. 16), and may well have had some sort of visible tree properties, which get involved in the subsequent action. The first ambush sequence apparently depended on a familiar stage property, indicated in the direction, '*Enter Faustus, with the false head*' (37.1 s.d.). His gown, also mentioned, may have helped conceal this device until Benvolio struck it off. The Knights' plans for mutilating Faustus's body are notably barbaric – nailing horns to his head, stuffing his eyeballs in his mouth – and ensure that audience sympathy remains with Faustus. When Faustus suddenly revives, his planned revenges are equally savage, but Frederick's rhyming proverbial tag at line 94 keeps the tone comic.

The second ambush, by the soldiers, is countered by Faustus's enchantment of the trees, which 'remove at [his] command' (l. 101), anticipating Birnam Wood in *Macbeth*. Faustus then 'strikes the door' to summon an army of devils, one playing a drum, accompanied by Mephistopheles with fireworks (105.1–3 s.d.). This conflict is perhaps the play's most elaborate and expensive spectacle, incorporating multiple actors, devil costumes, martial music, pyrotechnics, banners, weapons, and moving trees. It is followed by a comic coda in B. 4.3 when the hapless Knights, all now with horns on their heads, lament their disgrace and slink off to live in seclusion in the woods. The whole episode builds on chapters 30 and 31 of *The English Faust Book*, to which the adaptors certainly had access. None of it has much to do with the plot about Faustus's soul, though he does remind the audience, in 4.2.71–2, of his 24-year bargain.

A-text Act IV, scene i lines 100–195/B-text Act IV, scene iv

Following the Emperor scene in the A-text there is a rather sudden and significant transition, as Faustus begins to reflect on the expiration of his bargain, then carries out one of his lowliest pranks on the Horse-courser. It is not a new scene in the A-text – the action is continuous, with Faustus remaining onstage – but the style, tone, and even the location change substantially. The setting shifts, as the scene progresses, from the Emperor's court to the road to Wittenberg, and finally to Faustus's own house, where he sleeps in his chair. The B-text has a very similar scene as 4.4, also centered on the gulling of the Horse-courser, though it has a longer payoff that extends over several scenes. The hoaxes practiced on the Horse-courser – which use a disappearing horse and a false leg to gain a 40-dollar profit – bring Faustus down to the level of Robin the Ostler. Whatever high aims Faustus may have had for his powers, he seems to be frittering them away here. The triviality of these tricks (which nonetheless may be very entertaining) is counterpointed by reminders that Faustus's time is running out.

100–8   Faustus's grave and poetic meditations on mortality seem to come from nowhere after the merriment with the Knight. The apt adjective 'restless' applies not only to time, which runs on with 'calm and silent foot,' but to Faustus himself, as he turns his ceaseless wanderings back toward Wittenberg. The repetition of Mephistopheles's name in this surprisingly intimate conversation reminds us of his critical role in Faustus's story. For the past several scenes he has been merely an assistant or sidekick in Faustus's conjurings; here the familiar epithet 'Sweet Mephistopheles' suggests a more personal connection, though the audience will likely be conscious of the irony.

In offering Faustus a choice of transport, Mephistopheles employs the convention by which horses were avoided on the stage, but he also sets up the Horse-courser's overture. The mention of a 'fair and pleasant green' as the setting contributes to the somber sense of life's fleeting pleasures that gives depth to the scene.

109–17   The Horse-courser will be identified as a rustic yokel by his clothing, his manner of speech, and his comic mangling of Faustus's name. Since 'Fustian' means both fabric padding and, by extension, overinflated rhetoric, the name provides an ironic comment on Faustus as a wordy showman. The Horse-courser might himself have had negative associations for an Elizabethan audience. The horse-trading business had a reputation for shrewd and sometimes unethical practices that persists in modern usages. In going about to cheat someone who would probably cheat him, Faustus may be seen as having justice on his side; nonetheless, he may forfeit some audience sympathy through his haughty bargaining.

118–23   The Horse-courser enlists Mephistopheles's support for his cause, presumably believing him to be Faustus's servant. Is Mephistopheles still dressed as a friar at this point? He has been present, though presumably invisible, since the earlier part of the scene with the Emperor. Faustus refers to him as 'my boy,' and later the Horse-courser calls him his 'snipper-snapper' (l. 157). If Mephistopheles retains his earlier appearance, these condescending terms may be comically obtuse, and irritating to him; on the other hand he may have temporarily slipped into a new role, perhaps with appropriate livery. The B-text entirely omits Mephistopheles from the Horse-courser scene.

124–38   Faustus's warnings to the Horse-courser may be delivered in a tone of sly mischief; the audience will be in little doubt as to whether they will be heeded. The Horse-courser's eager aside reveals his greed, but there is a coarse, comic vitality in his suggestive 'hey ding ding' and his reference to the horse's 'buttock as slick as an eel.' Like most Elizabethan gulls, he runs headlong into his gulling (in this case literally), but he is not necessarily an unlikeable character. He contributes a welcome degree of earthiness and local color. His frankness in inquiring about the horse's urine provokes a squeamish rebuff from Faustus, but probably a laugh from the audience.

139–44   Faustus's stark recognition of his doomed state marks a startling shift in the scene. An actor could perhaps suggest that these grim reflections have been occupying Faustus throughout his interaction with the Horse-courser, to which he has given only partial attention. On the other hand, the oscillation between farcical hijinks and growing dread is built into this section of the play; directors will need to define how these elements intersect in an audience's experience. Faustus switches to verse here, and his lines have a formal severity, exemplified by the balance of 'fatal time' and 'final end' and the pounding alliteration of line 141. Lines 142–4 can convey anxious longing, foolish overconfidence, willful self-deception, or any combination thereof.

144 s.d.   Faustus goes to '*Sleep in his chair*' – presumably backed up against a curtain, or over a trap-door, through which the extra leg can be inserted under his gown. Meanwhile the Horse-courser enters '*all wet, crying.*' The A-text has unusually full stage directions to clarify the farcical action of the scene.

145–58   The Horse-courser, soaked and furious, delivers a comic account of his gulling. His hostile reference to 'Doctor Lopus' alludes to Queen Elizabeth's physician Rodrigo Lopez, who was hanged in 1594 for allegedly attempting to poison the Queen. Since this occurred a year after Marlowe's death, the line (and perhaps the scene) is presumably a later addition. The Horse-courser's failure to heed Faustus's warnings – indeed, his certainty that they conceal desirable magical qualities in the horse – parallels Faustus's own ignoring of the Good Angel's admonitions and Mephistopheles's descriptions of hell. The speech is in breathless, exasperated prose, and the insistent repetition of the pronoun 'I' underlines the Horse-courser's self-centered indignation. The image of the bewildered Horse-courser in the pond, suddenly straddling a bundle of hay in place of Faustus's enchanted horse, is hilariously conjured by the speech, an instance of the power of description on the early modern stage. The whole monologue, spoken directly to the audience, is effectively an example of Elizabethan stand-up comedy.

159–74   The Horse-courser's abrupt and disrespectful address to Mephistopheles adds to the humor. His threat about 'his glass windows' may indicate that Faustus is wearing spectacles, though it might also refer to the house in which Faustus is now imagined to be.

Mephistopheles responds as a loyal and protective servant, presumably a bit of role-playing for the benefit of the Horse-courser – though there may be an element of truth in the statement that Faustus has not slept for eight nights. Faustus's sleep here is probably feigned, part of the gulling of the Horse-courser, who vigorously tries to wake him by '*Holler[ing] in his ear,*' according to the A-text stage direction.

174 s.d.–89 The pulling off of Faustus's false leg should probably be as much of a surprise for the audience as for the Horse-courser, though our shock will likely turn to laughter. As with '*the false head*' in the B-text, the leg is probably a specially fabricated prop that is partly concealed under Faustus's garments until it is grotesquely torn away. Interestingly, the A-text stage direction, like several earlier ones, is an imperative instruction to the actor: '*Pull him by the leg, and pull it away*' (l. 174 s.d.). It is not obvious how Mephistopheles colludes in the trick of the false leg, though he has some instrumental role in most of Faustus's other feats of magic. When the leg is off, Mephistopheles plays along with the plot, threatening the Horse-courser and helping to extort more money from him (in the B-text, by contrast, Mephistopheles is absent). This is a very funny scene in performance, but it has some serious implications. The pulling off of the leg anticipates the dismemberment of Faustus by devils at the end of the play: if Faustus's 'mangled limbs' appear onstage at the end, as in the B-text (5.3.17), they will probably include the very same props used in these comic scenes. The trick played on the Horse-courser is a somewhat cruel one, against an unequal adversary, and may alienate the audience's sympathies. 'Faustus hath his leg again' sounds like a childish taunt, and his crowing laughter over having cheated the wretched Horse-courser out of 40 dollars is arguably one of Faustus's lowest moments.

190–5 Wagner enters to set up Faustus's next command performance, for the Duke of Vanholt. Faustus agrees to go and meet him, creating an awkward transition in the A-text, in which the Vanholt scene follows immediately. The B-text inserts an intervening comic scene.

B-text Act IV, scene v

This is a brief and somewhat redundant scene, much of it taken up with a recapitulation of the Horse-courser's gulling. The tavern setting affords opportunities for energetic revelry, and the scene introduces two characters, the Carter and the Hostess, who will play significant further roles in the B-text comedy.

1–19   The Carter's boisterous energy and coarse appetite are evident in his opening lines, with their focus on 'beer' and 'whores.' The lines also help establish the tavern setting, as the stage quickly fills with bustling comic characters. The Hostess is probably an instantly recognizable figure, wearing an apron and carrying a tankard or some such prop. Tavern scenes were common in Elizabethan plays, but were mostly denoted, not by some significant alteration of the stage, but by the entrance of an iconic figure such as the Hostess, and the use of a few handheld glasses (see *Elizabethan Stage Conventions*, 97). Robin makes comic attempts to avoid the Hostess, and then bluff his way into a beer when caught out. The scene brings Robin and his fellow Dick together with the other lower-class characters, all in opposition to Faustus and his magic.

20–34   The Carter's story of his tricking by Faustus is taken from the *Faust Book*. Whoever wrote these comic scenes was judicious about what episodes to stage, such as the leg-pulling, and what to relate verbally, such as the eating of the load of hay. The balance of visible stage magic and comic storytelling maintains theatrical interest. The choric response of the astonished auditors at line 32 is funny in itself, and Robin's ineffective attempt to relate an additional wonder may provoke a further laugh.

35–53   The repetition of the Horse-courser's story seems unnecessary and may be evidence of revision, but a good comic actor can get a lot of humor from the enthusiastic, embellished retelling of an oft-told tale (the A-text's 'pond' is here a 'great river'). The appreciative audience ('O brave doctor!') adds to the fun. The notion that the Horse-courser has kept the leg as a trophy, rather than throwing it into 'some ditch or other' (B. 4.4.39), also has comic value.

54–9   Robin's indignant assertion that he was turned into an ape could provoke bemused stares from his companions. Perhaps, like the peasant turned into a newt in *Monty Python and the Holy Grail*, he 'got better.' His anger against Faustus leads him to stir the crowd to seek out the doctor for revenge – after, of course, having a few more drinks.

Act IV, scene ii (B-text Act IV, scene vi)

The scene at the Vanholts' shows Faustus using his magic in a trivial way in order to ingratiate himself with the nobility. Producing out-of-season grapes for the pregnant Duchess seems a paltry use for Faustus's powers, though it does provide the occasion for an interesting disquisition on global weather patterns. In B, the scene continues into a showdown with the lower-class mob.

s.d. The A-text, which has this scene immediately after 4.1, apparently begins with Faustus and Mephistopheles onstage: the direction reads 'Enter to them the Duke and the Duchess.' This is confusing, in that the previous scene ended with Faustus leaving to visit the Vanholts, and there is an 'exeunt' marked in the text. If the two scenes were played in succession without the two principals leaving the stage, it would make a very unusual transition in an early modern play, a sort of temporal and spatial jump cut. The B-text's intervening tavern scene avoids this problem.

1–12 Whatever entertainment Faustus provides for the Duke has evidently already occurred – the B-text mentions a 'castle in the air' – and the scene's focus is on Faustus's performance for the Duchess. The Duchess of Vanholt is often a memorable figure in productions. She has fewer than a dozen lines, but as the only female character apart from the hostess, the paramour, Helen, and Lechery, she draws a lot of attention in performance. Her noble status and her pregnancy are both probably evident in her costuming. The discussion of her pregnancy gives her conversation with Faustus a degree of intimacy, and there may be an air of courtliness and flirtation in their exchange. The yearnings of pregnant women often have a sexual dimension in early modern literature (cf. Elbow's wife in *Measure for Measure*), and many directors have taken this impulse a step further in eroticizing the Duchess. John Barton added a whole series of double-entendres on words like 'ravish't,' 'mount,' and 'erect' to their dialog for the RSC in 1974, while Dominic Dromgoole, at the Globe in 2011, had Faustus magically produce the grapes from under her skirts.

13–17 Faustus sends Mephistopheles, who is presumably invisible to the Vanholts, to fetch the grapes, and he returns within a few lines; time enough, on the Elizabethan stage, to walk offstage to collect the prop. Given that he is ostensibly going all the way to the other side of the world, his travel must be understood to be more or less instantaneous teleportation; it takes Shakespeare's Puck 40 minutes to make a similar orbit, and a modern satellite more than twice that long. The ease with which Mephistopheles makes the trip will likely be conveyed by his manner in entering with the dish of fruit.

18–27 Faustus's explanation as to how he procured the grapes in winter provides an interesting instance of the early modern understanding of how the seasons function across the world; a relevant point in a play so concerned with astronomy. Faustus incorrectly focuses on the east/west hemispheric division rather than north and south, and the B-text further clouds the issue by discussing 'countries that lie far east, where they have fruit twice a year,' but the overall grasp of hemispheric seasonal variation corresponds to modern understanding. Modern audiences may reflect, momentarily, on the fact that fruit is available to us year-round precisely through this kind of swift international trade.

28–39 The Duchess' relishing of the grapes, and the Duke's encouragement of her to 'well reward this learnèd man,' allow further opportunities for salaciousness, especially in the A-text, where the characters go off together at this stage.

B-text lines 35–57

In the B-text there is a sudden interruption as '*The clowns bounce at the gate within*,' loudly banging on one of the doors from offstage. Probably they remain in the tiring house, perhaps partly visible through the door, as they '*call out to talk to Faustus*.' This stage direction is unusual, in that it calls for ad libbed lines with specific content. None of the printed lines given to the various intruders mentions Faustus, yet when asked by the Duke what they want, the servant replies, 'They all cry out to speak with Doctor Faustus' (l. 49). The clowns, evidently having fortified themselves with drink, are noisy and rude. Dick's lines are particularly vulgar; the 'fig' (l. 41) is an

obscene gesture, and the pun on 'commit with his father' is grossly
sexual (ll. 42–3). The Duke and Duchess may react with alarm or dis-
gust, but Faustus is unflappable, seeing the intruders as 'subject for a
merriment' (l. 55).

B-text lines 58–74

Only four clowns are specified in the entry direction, but they give
the impression of an angry mob of townspeople. Visually contrasted
with the elegant gentlefolk, perhaps armed with weapons of the
torch-and-pitchfork variety, they make themselves at home in the
Duke's house, calling for beer. Their behavior is so 'outrageous' (l. 58)
that some editors speculate that Faustus has charmed them so they
do not actually know where they are. More likely, his question (l. 63)
and the servant's (l. 65) are rhetorical. Faustus plays along with them,
and sends for beer with the Duke's consent. Exactly how the beer is
procured is a little unclear; the Hostess is directed to enter with it
later, at line 99, and it is possible she has come in with the others, and
goes off at this point with the servant to help carry glasses.

B-text lines 75–109

The Carter's laborious jesting about Faustus's supposed wooden leg
is dragged out for several lines, presumably to the sniggering delight
of his companions. Faustus refuses to rise to the bait. Finally, the
Horse-courser is emboldened to ask about it, and Faustus dramatically pulls up his gown to reveal his legs (all of this action provides
evidence about Faustus's costume, which is almost certainly a long
scholar's robe). The clowns once again produce a comic 'All' reaction, as at lines 32 and 47 of the tavern scene (B. 4.5); here the humor
comes partly from their mistaken assumption that if the doctor has
two legs now, he must have had three to start with.

B-text lines 110–25

Finally, Faustus disposes of the intruders by charming them dumb.
With what action he does this, and whether Mephistopheles has any
hand in it, will be up to the director, as will the manner of their exit.
The grateful Duke and Duchess end the scene, and close off the comic

section of the play. There is an irony in the Duke's final line; from this point forward, Faustus's 'artful sport' will no longer be able to 'drive all sad thoughts away' (l. 125).

Act V

Act V, scene i

This crucial scene, largely similar in the two texts, returns the play to unalloyed tragedy as Faustus nears his end. His conjuration of a spirit in the form of Helen of Troy occasions one of the most celebrated lyric passages in Renaissance literature, certainly the most famous speech in Marlowe's drama. Helen's seductive appeal is countered by the presence of the Old Man, another almost allegorical figure who makes a final plea for Faustus to repent. Faustus's rejection of the latter, and embrace of the former, perhaps marks the final, irrevocable step toward his damnation.

s.d.   While the A-text has Wagner entering alone, the B-text opens this scene with a startling stage direction: '*Thunder and Lightning. Enter Devils with covered dishes. Mephistopheles leads them into Faustus's study. Then enter Wagner.*' Covered dishes are often carried in Elizabethan plays to signify banquets, but the threatening sound effects and demonic attendants make this a singularly disturbing stage action. The desperate revelry of the doomed Faustus may suggest a blasphemous version of the Last Supper, at which Jesus ate with his apostles before his crucifixion. It is one of several grim parodies of Christ's Passion in this sequence.

1–8   Wagner's first line is chilling in its directness – perhaps especially so in the A-text, where it immediately follows the light-hearted scene with the Vanholts. However Wagner has been played up to now, as insolent servant or choric presenter, this speech sounds a new note of gravity. There may be some bitterness in the increasingly emotive verbs 'banquet and carouse and swill' that Wagner uses to characterize Faustus's feasting (l. 4). His speculations about the 'belly-cheer' of the offstage banquet may be reinforced with appropriate sound effects from the discovery space. The carousing Scholars enter, perhaps a little unsteadily, on the last lines of Wagner's speech. The stage direction calls vaguely for '*two or three*' Scholars, though the lines in both texts require three.

9–25   The first Scholar's slightly rambling prose speech may show the effects of the offstage partying – words like 'beautifullest' and 'admirablest' can be delivered with a hint of drunkenness. His reference to 'Helen of Greece' is quite accurate – Helen was, after all, from Sparta – and it is interesting that the familiar sobriquet 'Helen of Troy' never occurs in either text of the play. Both the Scholar and Faustus use the phrase 'that peerless dame of Greece,' and there can be little doubt as to who is meant.

26–35   The apparition of Helen '*passeth over the stage*,' accompanied by music; the B-text specifies that Mephistopheles brings her in, thus calling attention to her demonic origins. She may simply walk from one door to the other, or she may move among the Scholars and even interact with them, though she seems to have departed by the time the first Scholar speaks. Productions have made a very wide range of choices as to how Helen is represented – she has been a gauzy puppet, a nude actress painted gold, a male actor in drag, or a mere invisible phantom, among other manifestations. On Marlowe's stage she would have been a boy actor in a wig and dress, probably classical in appearance, possibly masked. To present the most beautiful woman in history is something of a staging challenge, though her allure is largely conveyed, of course, by the way other characters respond to her, by her graceful passage across the stage, and above all by the words in which Marlowe paints her beauty. The scene is full of superlatives and words of high degree: 'beautifullest,' 'admirablest,' 'peerless,' 'majesty' (three times), 'rich,' 'heavenly,' 'passeth all compare.' The Scholars' responses to Helen may range, in performance, from awestruck reverence to strip-club lasciviousness.

36–47   The Old Man first speaks just after the Scholars exit, though in the A-text he has been onstage since line 32, perhaps long enough to catch a glimpse of the demonic Helen. The staging may suggest that he is a kind of symmetrical opposite to her, just as the Good and Evil Angels are opposites in the *psychomachia* for Faustus's soul. Production choices will determine whether the Old Man comes across more as a real human character or an allegorical personification. He has elements of both, though Mephistopheles's later lines suggest that he does have a mortal body that can be afflicted. He may have robes or a staff suggestive of a religious affiliation; his age is likely conveyed by white hair or beard.

The Old Man's exhortation to Faustus differs in the two texts. The A version is shorter and more severe, both in its condemnation of Faustus's 'flagitious crimes of heinous sins' and in its emphasis on the 'Saviour sweet' whose 'blood alone can wash away thy guilt' (A. 44, 46, 47). The B-text's Old Man is more measured and more personal; he speaks to his 'gentle son' in 'tender love' and 'kind rebuke' (B. 47, 48, 50). The two texts suggest two different directions in which an actor could take the characterization, whichever text is used.

48–52   Faustus's immediate response is despair. With an emotional violence we have not seen since Act II, Faustus addresses himself in exclamations of frenzied condemnation. With startling swiftness, Mephistopheles is at his side, offering him a dagger. Mephistopheles may have been present throughout the scene, or he may suddenly re-enter to tempt Faustus to kill himself. The proffered dagger, as an inducement to suicide, was a familiar emblem in Tudor literature. In John Skelton's moral interlude *Magnificence*, Despair and Mischief offer the hero a knife and rope to kill himself; Marlowe has Techelles offer a dagger to Agydas in *Tamburlaine Part 1*; in Book I of *The Faerie Queene*, the personification of Despair offers a dagger to the Red Cross Knight. The threat of suicide here would have been instantly recognizable and morally clear to an Elizabethan audience.

53–62   The Old Man's pleas temporarily dissuade Faustus. He may literally see an angel over Faustus's head, if the Good Angel is present in the scene, or this may be an instance where the audience has to imagine that which is spoken of: a significant interpretive question for the final scenes of the play. Faustus claims to take comfort, at least momentarily, but the Old Man's despondent exit suggests that the comfort is illusory. Even the Old Man seems to despair of Faustus's 'helpless,' or 'hapless,' soul (A and B).

63–6   Faustus wrestles with his soul's predicament in four riveting lines. The balanced opposition of 'I do repent, and yet I do despair' captures the dilemma concisely; but even this brief formulation contains rhetorical ambiguity through which the actor of Faustus can define his situation in various ways. Are the clauses exactly parallel – does Faustus repent and despair at the same time and in the same way? Or is the 'do' of the first phrase emphatic and defensive, suggesting that Faustus is complaining, with an almost childish apprehension of unfairness, that his attempts at repentance do not alleviate his despair? Or, perhaps, is there a temporal division within the line, suggesting that Faustus can repent for awhile, but then slides back into despair? All of these possibilities, and more, are packed into this moment. The actor must also consider to whom he delivers these lines, or parts of them: to the audience, to the exiting Old Man, to Mephistopheles, to himself?

In the following line, Faustus recapitulates the problem in a more graphic and physical way, as a war within his breast carried out by the forces of hell and grace – another version of the *psychomachia*. Whether Goethe knew Marlowe's version or not, he expressed this same idea in one of his Faust's most famous lines, about having two souls warring within his breast (*Faust Part I*, 'Before the Gate'). For Goethe's Faust, they are his own impulses toward earthly pleasure and divine knowledge; Marlowe's line suggests a conflict between external forces carried out within Faustus, leaving him a wasted battleground.

67–75 Mephistopheles aggressively castigates Faustus, using the language of treason and arrest; Faustus immediately capitulates in terms of loyalty and pardon. This use of political language for a spiritual relationship would have had special meaning for Elizabethan audiences. A spectator at the original production of *Doctor Faustus* who had attained the age of 60 would have had the official state religion change four times during his or her lifetime. Anyone taking office under the Queen still had to swear an Oath of Supremacy declaring allegiance to her in spiritual as well as political matters. Faustus offers to reconfirm his oath to Lucifer 'With my blood,' and Mephistopheles urges him to do so quickly. It may be that Faustus actually cuts his arm with Mephistopheles's dagger, and perhaps even writes again on a document, as in Act II. There does not seem to be much time for stage action here, so it may be that the blood oath is carried out in a different way this time. On the other hand, Faustus could be writing while the dialog proceeds about the Old Man and

Helen. If so, the props of the desk, quill, paper, and so forth, would need to be easily accessible, probably in the 'study' of the discovery space.

76–81 Faustus's desire for Mephistopheles to torment the Old Man is strikingly cruel but psychologically plausible. Faustus displaces his own suffering onto another, perhaps envious and resentful of the Old Man's condition of grace. The terse simplicity of Mephistopheles's reply at line 79 conveys the power of the faith Faustus has rejected. Like many of Mephistopheles's other most potent utterances, such as 'Why this is hell, nor am I out of it,' the force of the line comes from its almost matter-of-fact frankness, its ability to sum up gigantic metaphysical questions in a few stark words. Mephistopheles returns to a kind of blasé weariness in agreeing to afflict the poor Old Man with physical tortures; his recognition that these will be 'of little worth' does not necessarily erase the chilling nature of these lines.

82–90 Faustus turns his thoughts from the Old Man to Helen, again suggesting the opposition of these two figures. What makes Faustus desire her at this moment? We may recall how, in Act II, he made 'sweet pleasure conquer deep despair' by having Homer sing to him of 'Alexander's [Paris's] love,' in other words Helen; she seems to have been a touchstone for him throughout the play.

90 s.d. Helen's second entrance is a show-stopping moment. Probably she is in some way summoned or brought in by Mephistopheles. The B-text specifies, remarkably, that she should be *'passing over between two cupids.'* This suggests some masque-like procession, or something along the lines of the apparition of Venus in a Renaissance painting. It is hard to imagine a modern production employing two cupids without an effect of Vegas-style excess and absurdity; but perhaps that is not out of place here. If Helen is not, after all, a beautiful mortal woman but a demonic instance of Faustus's gross self-delusion, she might not necessarily appear to the audience as a figure of surpassing beauty. In two major twentieth-century productions, Ian McKellen embraced a wispy puppet, and Jude Law narcissistically kissed his own reflection in a mirror. The 2015 American Shakespeare Center production made a startling choice by having the female actor of

Mephistopheles transform into Helen onstage by slipping off her friar's robe and embracing Faustus.

91–2 The play's most famous lines present the same challenge of overfamiliarity as Hamlet's 'To be or not to be,' Lady Bracknell's 'A handbag?', or Stanley Kowalski's 'Stella!'. Audiences will be listening, with one ear, to the voices of past actors, or their own imagined performances, before the actor has a chance to complete the line. It may have been the same for Edward Alleyn, when he played the role in the repertory of the Admiral's Men. The phrase about 'the face that launched a thousand ships' seems to have been immediately popular, and was frequently quoted, copied, or parodied by other Elizabethan writers. Shakespeare, for instance, uses a version of it in *Troilus and Cressida*, his play about the Trojan War. The 1996 film *Shakespeare in Love* includes an amusing sequence where an exasperated Shakespeare, holding auditions for *Romeo and Juliet*, must listen to actor after actor performing Faustus's 'thousand ships' lines. Breathtaking and familiar as these lines are, the actor must find a way to generate them in the moment, in response to his vision of Helen.

93–7 This kiss, and the lines surrounding it, are filled with implications for our understanding of the play. W. W. Greg argued in 1946 that by kissing and presumably copulating with the succubus representing Helen, Faustus is making himself guilty of the sin of demoniality (sex with a devil), and therefore finally, irrevocably damning himself. Other scholars have disagreed, arguing that demoniality would still have been considered a pardonable sin, but the lines about Helen making Faustus 'immortal' and her lips 'suck[ing] forth his soul' suggest damnation. The line 'give me my soul again' – which seems to have been remembered by Shakespeare in writing the first meeting of Romeo and Juliet – also supports the notion that Faustus is giving up his soul in kissing Helen. Interestingly, the B-text's Faustus says 'Heaven is in these lips,' whereas in A he says 'Heaven *be* in these lips,' a subjunctive with the suggestion of an imperative. The B-reading could reinforce the idea that Faustus trades heaven for Helen, or imply that he is seeking a kind of salvation in her kiss.

  The lines certainly suggest that Faustus and Helen kiss (twice, at least), but the actors have choices to make about the sensuality of the kisses, the degree of responsiveness from Helen, and the

physical positioning of the actors. It should also be remembered that
in Marlowe's theatre Helen would have been a boy actor. Marlowe
was associated with male–male sexuality, and was not shy of depicting kissing in his work – Edward and Gaveston kiss in *Edward II*, for
instance, as do Mortimer and the Queen, who would have been a
male actor. But a kiss is a powerful act onstage, whoever is involved,
and the kisses between Faustus and Helen will likely be a memorable
moment in any performance.

98–110   At this point, in the A-text, the Old Man enters to see
Faustus and Helen together; he does not reappear in the B version.
Faustus's speech (essentially identical in the two texts) proceeds with
an odd fantasy of re-enacting the Trojan War, with himself in the
role of Paris; it is indicative of Faustus's self-destructiveness that he
would cause the sack of his own city of Wittenberg. The speech is
composed of sonorous blank-verse lines, grouped in twos and fours.
It lacks the rising build of some of Marlowe's other great set pieces,
such as Tamburlaine's paeans to beauty and power, or Faustus's long
speeches in Act I. The language is rich with evocative classical names,
and with images of brightness, beauty, and the sky, but the speech is
by no means wholly positive. Some of the associations are violent –
the stories of Semele and Arethusa invoke sexuality as a destructive
power. Even the loveliest lines have a poignancy about them, as in the
image of 'the evening air/ clad in the beauty of a thousand stars.' The
final line has an uncompromising fervor typical of Marlowe's overreaching heroes, but it begins with a negative – it is not about what
will be, but what will not be.

How does Faustus play this speech? Is it an intimate love scene
with Helen, a smarmy seduction, or perhaps a desperate plea to an
unattainable phantom? What does Helen do while Faustus speaks?
Does she proceed across the stage, as '*passing over*' implies, perhaps
leaving before he finishes speaking to her? Do Faustus and Helen
leave together, and where do they go? How explicit are the sugges-
tions that they are going to bed together? In the B-text, the scene ends
with their exit.

111–19   In the A-text the Old Man remains onstage, condemning
Faustus for excluding grace from his soul – and by implication, perhaps, for damning himself through sex with the succubus representing

Helen. Devils enter to threaten him – perhaps the supernumerary fiends who will later drag Faustus to hell, or possibly Mephistopheles, Lucifer, and Beelzebub. Their assaults may be frightening to the audience, and even painful to the Old Man, but evidently they have limited effect, as Mephistopheles had predicted at line 81. When the Old Man says 'see how the heavens smiles/At your repulse' (ll. 117–18), he presumably gestures upwards, but whether the audience is meant to see anything of this divine reaction is not clear from the text.

Act V, scene ii

The climactic scene of Faustus's torment and damnation is one of the high points of early modern drama. It reveals the soul-searching power of the soliloquy convention, and features some of Marlowe's greatest poetry as Faustus undergoes a terrifying vigil and makes his final, fruitless efforts to evade his fate. This great speech is preceded by a moving colloquy of Faustus and his fellow Scholars, as well as, in the B-text, a revelation of the diabolical conspiracy against Faustus. The final moments of Faustus's exit into hell revitalize a familiar emblem from medieval drama with the full panoply of Renaissance stage effects.

B-text lines 1–26

The B-text precedes the main action of 5.2 with a short prelude in which the chief devils gloat over their future victims, 'Those souls which sin seals the black sons of hell' (l. 3; note the sinister, sibilant hiss of the repeated *s*-sounds). The audience may well feel itself included in this group of the devils' 'subjects.' Lucifer speaks of 'ascend[ing],' which may suggest that he and the other devils appear in the gallery above the stage (as they may have done in the B-text's 1.3). If so, it would reverse the usual cosmic structure of the Elizabethan stage, in which the heavens were above and hell below. On the other hand, nothing in the text insists that the devils be above; they may simply walk out onto the main stage or even climb out of the trap, which would make sense of 'ascend' another way. The devils' entry is made more threatening by the sound of thunder. John Melton's 1620 pamphlet *The Astrologaster* refers to a production of *Doctor Faustus* in which 'shag-haired devils run roaring over the stage with squibs in their mouths, while drummers make thunder in the tiring house and the twelve-penny hirelings make artificial lighting in their heavens.' This description gives some sense of how this scene might have appeared to an early modern audience.

Mephistopheles's line 8 establishes that the setting is understood to be Faustus's study. His predictions about Faustus's behavior give a clue as to the psychology of the upcoming speech, in which 'his laboring brain' will beget 'idle fantasies/To overreach the devil' (ll. 13–15). As Faustus enters, a brief exchange with Wagner establishes his morbid mindset, mentioned in Wagner's earlier speech. One of the Scholars comments that Faustus's 'looks are changed,' perhaps suggesting a significant contrast between the way Faustus appears and behaves here compared to the previous Helen scene.

Lines 1–64 (B-text lines 27–89)

The scene with the Scholars is nearly identical in the two texts. Faustus's longest scene in prose, it provides a rare glimpse of him as part of a human community; he calls the first Scholar his 'sweet chamber-fellow' (B. 29). The Scholars, who may before have been comic caricatures, show astonished concern and sympathy for their despairing colleague. Faustus is struck by abrupt premonitions of his doom that break forth in repeated, staccato phrases: 'Look sirs, comes he not? Comes he not?', 'Hell, ah, hell forever!', 'I would lift up my hands, but see, they hold them, they hold them!' Whether any physical restraint is placed on Faustus by the devils is up to the director, but it is probably more powerful for his ravings to be purely hallucinatory. Scenes of guilt and madness in the Elizabethan theatre often feature a recoiling from fearful visions unseen by the audience; the death of Cardinal Beaufort in Shakespeare's *2 Henry VI* is one such example, the 'flaws and starts' of Macbeth and his wife another.

The Scholars, aghast, finally get an explanation for Faustus's bizarre behavior, and though the audience is well aware of the situation, the blunt avowals of 'I gave them my soul' and 'I wrote them a bill with mine own blood' can still have the force of startling revelations. The simple, parallel statements of lines 42–3 have similar power, and anticipate the rhythms of Faustus's final monologue. The third Scholar's momentary determination to stay with Faustus can be a touching impulse, no less so for his being quickly dissuaded from it by the threat of divine wrath.

B-text lines 90–135

While the A-text proceeds directly to Faustus's last speech, the B-text includes a lengthy episode revisiting the supernatural machinery of Faustus's story, and foretelling his sufferings in hell. The language changes back to verse for the remainder of the play. Mephistopheles's gloating over Faustus's damnation can come across as a shocking betrayal, even though the audience should hardly be surprised by it. The explicit assertion that Mephistopheles obstructed Faustus 'when thou wert i'the way to heaven' can be deeply disturbing, and has implications for the theology of the play. Did Faustus truly never have a chance to repent? The detail about Mephistopheles turning the pages of the Bible, and leading Faustus's eye away from promises of salvation, recalls the incomplete scriptural passages Faustus dismissed at the beginning of the play. Is it possible that the supernatural conspiracy was already in place against him, even then? Mephistopheles's triumphant and jocular crowing over Faustus's destruction will probably generate some sympathy for Faustus even for audiences who feel he has deserved his fate. The text marks an exit here for Mephistopheles. Perhaps he leaves to rejoin Lucifer and Beelzebub in the gallery to oversee Faustus's final damnation, perhaps he participates in it – or this may be his final exit from the play. Even if he leaves now, his presence continues to haunt the play: Faustus's last word will be 'Mephistopheles.'

The Good and Bad Angels enter 'at several doors,' at opposite sides at the back of the stage. Their first four speeches interlock through shared lines – the words of the Bad Angel fill out the beats of the iambic pentameter, completing the pattern the Good Angel's lines begin. This use of shared short lines is rare in this play, and in Marlowe generally, and here gives the sense of the Bad Angel's mocking words gleefully snapping at the heels of the Good Angel's more measured and sorrowful speeches. This duet of the Angels also uses more rhyming verse than has appeared before. Rhyme feels appropriate to the moralizing tone of the passage. Most English drama from its origins until Marlowe's generation was written in rhyme, and much was of a religious or moral character. Marlowe himself was one of the noted exponents of unrhymed blank verse, and began the prologue to Tamburlaine by setting himself apart 'From jigging veins of rhyming mother wits.' The strong use of rhyme in this section (whoever wrote it) matches up with the rather old-fashioned, morality-play aspects of the two Angels' pronouncements.

The unusual stage direction '*Music while the throne descends*' suggests that some sort of celestial chair property was lowered from the trap-door in the heavens above the stage. The Angel's lines reference 'yonder throne' as well as some 'bright shining saints,' but such things could easily be conjured by the audience's imagination as the actor described them – a common enough practice in the Elizabethan theatre. The stage direction seems, however, to give the throne a concrete reality. Henslowe paid carpenters for 'making the throne in the heavens' in 1595, so it may be that these lines were added to highlight the new stage effect. A later playwright, Ben Jonson, mocked the device whereby a 'creaking throne comes down, the boys to please,' (*Every Man in His Humour*, Prologue, 16), but in the 1590s it may have been a spectacular moment.

At what is literally the eleventh hour, the Good Angel finally abandons Faustus. His valediction, while not unexpected, can be painful in effect. One might compare the ending of the morality play *Everyman*, where even the hero's positive qualities depart at his graveside, but his Good Deeds accompany him to the afterlife.

When the Good Angel says 'The jaws of hell are open to receive thee,' there is probably some change in the stage, corresponding to the direction '*Hell is discovered*.' Possibly the trap-door opens, though that would seem to create a significant distraction, and maybe a danger, for the actor of Faustus as he goes through his long monologue. Perhaps a curtain is drawn in the discovery space, to reveal a graphic representation of the horrors of hell, such as those depicted by Renaissance artists like Giotto, Bosch, and Breughel. The Rose theatre may have used a 'hell-mouth' like those employed in medieval drama – Henslowe's inventory of props includes one. The Bad Angel's speech features a number of vivid details about hell's torments, and these might have been somehow visually represented to the audience; but they need not have been. An actor's compelling delivery, and Faustus's reactions, can make this scene perfectly terrifying without a single pitchfork, red light, or wisp of smoke. Nonetheless, this scene raises real questions about how, and how much, the supernatural dimensions of the play were represented in the theatre.

64 s.d. '*The clock strikes eleven.*' Does Faustus wait for all 11 peals to pass before beginning his speech? Such a pause – up to 30 seconds or so – would be a bold choice in the theatre, but the tension of the scene might justify it. The fact that Faustus's opening line is only three beats long suggests a pause preceding it. The tolling bell, and the passing hour it represents, structures Faustus's monologue, and gives it tremendous dramatic power. The speech constantly reminds the audience of the passing of time in the theatre – not something plays usually strive to do. The whole speech probably takes 3–5 minutes in a typical performance, and can make the audience feel the swiftness with which Faustus's last hour passes, or the slow and steady approach of his doom.

Faustus's final monologue is a long and challenging one. It formally balances the soliloquy at the beginning, and between them they comprise around one-sixth of the role in the A-text. Coming at the end of a long and difficult role, this speech demands great emotional intensity and vocal stamina. Probably the actor is alone onstage, unless the devils are lurking somewhere. He may speak mostly to the audience, but in fact many of his lines are addressed to different hearers, real or imagined. At different points, he speaks to himself, to his body and soul; to the sun, the earth, and his stars; to God and Christ, Lucifer and Mephistopheles; and finally to adders, serpents, and 'ugly hell.'

65–73 The first nine lines of the speech (which is very similar in the two texts) address the passing of time. Faustus calls on the celestial movements that mark time to cease, or to allow the time allotted him to expand. Marlowe's verse – and it is almost certainly Marlowe's at this point of the play – becomes freer and more creative in this passage, subtly varying the regular, end-stopped, 10-beat lines that have been the norm throughout the work. The enjambment of lines 70–1, like a wave cresting and breaking, conveys Faustus's hopeless longing for 'Perpetual day.' Faustus's desperation is expressed in the ever-decreasing units by which he hopes to extend his hour: 'A year, a month, a week, a natural day.' This is great poetry – the repeated pattern broken by the poignant 'natural' – but it is also psychologically astute: it is the 'bargaining' of the terminal patient, as described by psychiatrist Elisabeth

Kübler-Ross in her influential book *On Death and Dying*. The irony that Faustus believes he could do in a day what he has been unable to do in 24 years – 'repent, and save his soul' – does not decrease the searing pathos of this moment.

74   This line is taken from Ovid's *Amores*, which Marlowe had translated. In the poem, the line calls for the horses of the night to run slowly, so the speaker will not have to rise from the bed of his beloved. This was a celebrated phrase that at least some educated Elizabethans would have recognized from their schooldays. There is obviously an extreme irony in Marlowe's, and Faustus's, use of it here. For modern audiences, as for a majority of Marlowe's, the line will not convey this level of meaning, but an actor can put a great level of emotion into these Latin words.

75–6   Simple parallel phrases, five in two lines, give an inevitability to Faustus's damnation. Apart from Faustus's name, all these words would have been pronounced as monosyllables (as 'devil' generally was in Elizabethan drama), adding to the relentless rhythm of the lines. The shift in the verbs, from the present tense of time and the stars, to the future of the clock and the devil, to the emphatic 'must' of Faustus's damnation, tells the story of the speech in a nutshell.

77–9   Suddenly Faustus generates a burst of energy, probably expressed in a violent gestural movement upwards. The vision of Christ's blood streaming in the firmament is one of Marlowe's most memorable lines, though it is absent from the B-text, possibly because of its theological implications. In the Rose theatre, Alleyn's Faustus may have looked up toward the heavens above the stage, or the actual open sky above the heads of the audience. Many of them may have looked up too.

80–5   In calling on Christ, Faustus feels, or imagines that he feels, the resentful devils tearing his heart. As soon as he calls on Lucifer, the vision of Christ's blood disappears, and is replaced with an angry and threatening God. All explicit mentions of God are cut from the B-text, presumably because of the 1606 Act to Restrain Abuses of Players, which forbade the naming of God onstage; oddly, the references to Christ remain.

86–95 Faustus tries to escape God's wrath by calling on the mountains to cover him, in lines echoing the Bible (Hosea 10:8; Revelations 6:16). The 'No, no?' stands as a line by itself in the A-text, perhaps signaling a hopeful, then disappointed pause; B puts in a single 'No' at the head of the next line. Faustus may physically fling himself to the ground, literally attempting to 'headlong run into the earth.' After this fails, he invokes the astrological influences on his birth, blaming them for his damnation, and begs them to destroy his body through thunder and lightning and thus purify his soul. This is difficult but dynamic metaphysical language, challenging for an actor to make an audience follow precisely, but building powerfully through successive lines, and loaded with vivid images: 'foggy mist,' 'labouring cloud,' 'vomit forth,' 'smoky mouths.'

95 s.d.–97 The clock strikes, probably a single peal marking the half hour. The A-text uses two short lines, the B-text a single long one, to express Faustus's recognition of the passage of time. The former suggests a slow realization, the latter breathless panic.

98–104 Faustus, having given up on salvation, enters another stage of 'bargaining' as he desperately wishes for a finite period to his suffering. By contrast with line 72, Faustus's rhetoric here amplifies time rather than contracting it. Faustus confronts the implications of eternity with the stark realization of line 104. The 'Oh' that begins the line is extrametrical, and absent from the B-text. It may be an actor's addition, though both versions of the speech have multiple instances of the interjections 'Oh,' 'O,' and 'Ah' (14 in A, 12 in B). These sounds, common in early modern texts, give an actor the opportunity to express inarticulate emotion, beyond what can be conveyed in words. This passage obviously contains a great deal of such feeling for Faustus, and invites the actor to use these sounds to communicate his suffering in the most elemental, preverbal manner.

105–12 In invoking 'Pythagoras' metempsychosis,' Marlowe is indulging his love for exotic-sounding language, but also alluding to the classical doctrine of the transmigration of souls, revived by Renaissance Neoplatonists. Faustus longs to be transformed into a 'brutish beast,' and to have his soul 'dissolved in elements.'

The yearning for dissolution is a theme throughout the speech; cf. the 'foggy mist' earlier and the air and water of the final lines.

113–15   Faustus's cursing – of his parents, himself, and Lucifer – allows the actor an explosive outburst of anger to balance the fear and misery explored earlier in the speech. Faustus's cursing his parents recalls Job's cursing the day of his birth (3:1), one of many Biblical echoes in the speech.

115 s.d.   The striking of the clock begins here, and probably continues through the remainder of the speech; Faustus's line seems to respond immediately to the first peal of the bell. Depending on the timing, the bell could finish around the time the devils take Faustus away. The A-text calls for 'Thunder and lightning' two lines after the bell begins; the B-text has thunder accompany the devils' entry. Either way, the bell and the thunder create a powerful sonic backdrop to Faustus's last lines, one that will create a memorable atmosphere but also a vocal challenge for the actor.

116–20   Faustus's wish for his body to turn to air and his soul to 'little waterdrops' continue the leitmotif of dissolution. Line 120 again invokes a threatening, angry God. The line also recalls Jesus' last words on the Cross, 'My God, my God, why hast thou forsaken me?' (Mark 15:34). There have been ironic references to Christ's Passion throughout the play (cf. '*Consummatum est*' when Faustus signs the contract in 2.3). Faustus's vigil in his study might be compared to the Agony in the Garden, in which Jesus anticipates his crucifixion, so it is perhaps appropriate that he should here echo Jesus' final words.

120 s.d.–123   The A-text stage direction here specifies '*Enter devils*' (in B, they enter a line earlier accompanied by thunder). How many devils, how and from where they enter, and whether Mephistopheles or Lucifer are among them, are among the many questions directors will need to answer in staging this scene. In the Rose theatre, the most likely places for Faustus's final exit were the trap and the discovery space. It is probable that Marlowe's Faustus was dragged off physically by a number of devil-actors, though the scene could conceivably be performed with Faustus alone onstage, and exiting under his own power (or disappearing in a blackout). But an Elizabethan performance would almost certainly have taken full advantage of the range of early modern stage effects: the sound of the bells and thunder, terrifying masks and costumes for the devils, pyrotechnical effects for hell, and some sort of final, spectacular disappearance through a trap or hell-mouth. The line 'ugly hell, gape not' suggests a visible space, newly disclosed. Faustus's final line, perhaps spoken as he is carried off, is doubly poignant. He wishes, in a last, desperate attempt to save himself, to burn the books that have helped define him from the first moment. And his dying cry is to the demon who has been his companion and tormentor. How does Faustus speak this final 'Ah, Mephistopheles'? Is it a roar of physical agony, a sudden recognition, a wail of longing? Is Mephistopheles present, and does he respond? How do the principal characters of the play make their exit from it?

Act V, scene iii B-text

The B-text adds another scene at this point, as the Scholars return from the other room to discover Faustus's torn remains. Are the limbs flung out from wherever the devils exit, or concealed somewhere in Faustus's study? The limbs seem to be crucial properties in the scene, as the language repeatedly calls attention to them: '*See, here* are Faustus limbs,' '…have torn him *thus.*' Staging this moment risks undesired audience laughter, but perhaps the grotesquerie is deliberate. This episode has a clear source in the *Faust Book*, where the Scholars find Faustus's hall 'besprinkled with blood, his brains cleaving to the wall' and his battered body parts tossed throughout the house. The representation of a torn body onstage has a long dramatic history, from the *sparagmos* of the classical tragedy *The Bacchae* through medieval works like the Croxton *Play of the Sacrament*, in which a would-be defiler of the Host has his hand torn off. One might add to this list the actual bodies of beheaded and quartered traitors, dismembered in theatrical public spectacles. The dismemberment of Faustus restages the earlier comic episodes of the false leg and the false head (perhaps using the same props), and also recalls Faustus's desire for his limbs to 'issue from [the] smoky mouths' of the clouds in the preceding speech. To be sure, many directors, even those using the B-text, cut this scene in performance, and many scholars have argued against its Marlovian authenticity. But it seems to me there are good reasons for considering staging it. The scene shows the community of Scholars grappling with Faustus's dangerous course, extending a theme first raised in 1.2. It recapitulates the horrific events of the night from a different perspective, vividly evoking the 'shrieks and cries' and the 'house … all on fire.' And it presents a sympathetic remembrance of Faustus, 'once admired/For wondrous knowledge,' that matches up well with the sentiments with which the final chorus begins. Presumably the Scholars collect some of the larger pieces of the corpse, and exit gravely to 'give his mangled limbs due burial.'

Epilogue

The play ends, as it began, with the Chorus. The final speech is identical in the two texts. A lone actor walks onto the stage and delivers to the audience a summing-up of the tragedy of Faustus, and an exhortation about how we should learn from it. Epilogues were not uncommon on the Elizabethan stage, though not as common as prologues. This is the only one in Marlowe's plays.

The first three lines acknowledge Faustus's lost potential with metaphors from the natural world. The harsh verbs 'cut' and 'burnèd' recall the destruction of Faustus's body and soul, but the images of the branch and the bough, together with the allusions to Apollo and learning, set up a counter-text that softens the overall effect. The language suggests that Faustus is to be mourned as well as condemned. Much depends on the actor's delivery and the characterization of the speaker. If it is Wagner, for instance, one can imagine him gloating a little over his newly inherited wealth, and adding an element of cynicism to his laments for Faustus. A more traditional Chorus, in a black robe associating him with the Scholars, or even wearing a laurel bough himself, might convey a more sympathetic assessment.

In any event, the second half of the chorus speech turns from praise to preaching; here the Chorus takes on the role of the morality-play 'Doctor,' who expounded the lesson of a medieval drama. After the stark statement that 'Faustus is gone,' the speaker goes on to pronounce on the meaning of his demise, and the way it should affect our behavior. Even in this apparently straightforward moral, however, there is ambiguity. 'Whose,' in line 5, refers to Faustus, and in line 7 to 'unlawful things,' but an audience might hear them, at least initially, as parallel statements, both pointing back to Faustus – in which case the second seems to contradict the first, allowing us to be at least momentarily 'enticed' by the 'deepness' of Faustus and his forbidden practices. The way the last line is spoken can suggest an orthodox condemnation of Faustus, or an indictment of the limitations placed by God on humanity, a bitterness about 'what heavenly power permits.'

The closing moments of any stage production have a great impact on its overall meaning for an audience. The cadences of the Chorus' final lines, the way he leaves the stage, the effects produced by music or (in the modern theatre) lighting, the last image the audience sees: all these will condition our understanding of what we have experienced. The final element of the text, in both versions, is not a spoken line nor a stage direction, but a conventional closing tag in Latin: 'Terminat hora diem; terminat author opus.' The hour ends the day; the author ends his work. While traditional, this phrase can have specific meaning with regard to Faustus, whose work has ended with the last hour of his last day. Or perhaps the author is God, or Mephistopheles, or Marlowe. In any event, the phrase is so suggestive that some productions have found ways to incorporate it into the performance. It is worth reflecting on, as this consideration of Doctor Faustus as a performance text comes to its own close.

3   Intellectual and Cultural Context

Marlowe's life and beliefs

Marlowe was a controversial figure in his own lifetime and has remained one since. His plays, with their subversive and aspiring heroes, are inevitably read alongside his own short and stormy life. As well as being a successful poet and playwright, he was allegedly an atheist, a homosexual, and a spy, and he died violently in mysterious circumstances at the age of 29. Like Faustus, Marlowe seems to have been a man of dangerous beliefs, religious skepticism, and sensual indulgence; like Faustus, he became, in his death, a moral emblem for his contemporaries. A brief sketch of his biography will provide context for important documents relating to his life and death.

Christopher Marlowe was born in Canterbury in 1564, the same year as Shakespeare. He was the son of a shoemaker, but was well educated at the King's School and won a scholarship to Cambridge where he took BA and MA degrees. There was some controversy over the granting of his MA, but the Privy Council sent a letter referring to his service 'on matters touching the benefit of his country,' and the degree was duly granted. It has been speculated that he worked for Francis Walsingham's secret service, perhaps as a double agent ferreting out Catholic plotters against the Queen.

Shortly after receiving his MA, Marlowe established himself as a writer in London, where *Tamburlaine the Great* was first performed in 1587. A second part of *Tamburlaine* followed, along with *Dido Queen of Carthage* (perhaps written at Cambridge), *Doctor Faustus*, *The Jew of Malta*, *Edward II*, and *The Massacre at Paris*. All of these but *Dido* were performed by the Lord Admiral's Men, led by Edward Alleyn and Philip Henslowe. Marlowe also wrote narrative and lyric poems, most notably *Hero and Leander* and *The Passionate Shepherd to His Love*, and translated classical texts.

Marlowe had several run-ins with the authorities in which scandalous opinions and behavior were attributed to him. Another apparent double agent, Richard Baines, accused Marlowe of counterfeiting coins, and later wrote an account of Marlowe's alleged heresies for the Privy Council and the Queen. It includes accusations of heresy, blasphemy, and homosexuality, as well the statement that 'the beginning of religion was only to keep men in awe': a sentiment similar to that expressed by Marlowe's Machiavelli, the prologue to *The Jew of Malta*, who says 'I count religion but a childish toy,/And hold there is no sin but ignorance.' The subversive statements alleged in the Baines Note, whether actually made by Marlowe or not, provide an interesting analog to the heterodox views of Marlowe's renegade heroes, including Faustus.

'A note containing the opinion of one Christopher Marly concerning his damnable judgment of religion, and scorn of God's word' by Richard Baines (1593)

That the Indians, and many authors of antiquity, have assuredly written of above 16 thousand years agone, whereas Adam is proved to have lived within 6 thousand years.

He affirmeth that Moses was but a juggler, and that one Hariot being Sir Walter Raleigh's man can do more than he.

That Moses made the Jews to travel 40 years in the wilderness (which journey might have been done in less than 1 year) ere they came to the promised land, to the intent that those who were privy to many of his subtleties might perish, and so an everlasting superstition reign in the hearts of the people.

That the beginning of religion was only to keep men in awe.

That it was an easy matter for Moses being brought up in all the arts of the Egyptians to abuse the Jews, being a rude and gross people.

That Christ was a bastard and his mother dishonest.

That he was the son of a carpenter, and that if the Jews among whom he was born did crucify him, they best knew him and whence he came.

That Christ deserved better to die than Barabas, and that the Jews made a good choice, though Barabas were both a thief and a murderer.

That if there be any God or any good religion, then it is in the Papists, because the service of God is performed with more ceremonies, as elevation of the mass, organs, singing men, shaven crowns, etc. That all Protestants are hypocritical asses.

That if he were put to write a new religion, he would undertake both a more excellent and admirable method, and that all the New Testament is filthily written.

That the woman of Samaria and her sister were whores and that Christ knew them dishonestly.

That Saint John the Evangelist was bedfellow to Christ and leaned always in his bosom; that he used him as the sinners of Sodoma.

That all they that love not tobacco and boys are fools.

That all the apostles were fishermen and base fellows, neither of wit nor worth; that Paul only had wit, but he was a timorous fellow in bidding men to be subject to magistrates against his conscience.

That he had as good a right to coin as the Queen of England, and that he was acquainted with one Poole, a prisoner in Newgate, who hath great skill in mixture of metals, and having learned some things of him, he meant through help of a cunning stamp-maker to coin French crowns, pistolets, and English shillings.

That if Christ would have instituted the sacrament with more ceremonial reverence, it would have been in more admiration; that it would have been better much better being administered in a tobacco pipe.

That the angel Gabriel was bawd to the Holy Ghost, because he brought the salutation to Mary.

That one Richard Cholmley hath confessed that he was persuaded by Marlowe's reasons to become an atheist.

Marlowe's death

While he was under investigation for heresy, Marlowe spent a day at an inn in Deptford in the company of three men who were all associated with the Elizabethan secret service. Marlowe allegedly got into a fight over the tavern bill or 'reckoning' with one of the men, Ingram Frizer. Frizer claimed Marlowe attacked him, and in the ensuing struggle he stabbed Marlowe over the eye with his own dagger. Frizer was pardoned by the Queen, and the episode of Marlowe's death, much augmented and distorted, became a common moral exemplum of the dangers of atheism. Beard's account, though clearly erroneous in some respects ('in London streets'), is the first printed version of Marlowe's death.

From *The Theatre of God's Judgments* by Thomas Beard (1597)

Not inferior to any of the former in atheism and impiety, and equal to all in manner of punishment was one of our own nation, of fresh and late memory, called Marlin [Marlowe], by profession a scholar, brought up from his youth in the University of Cambridge, but by practice a play-maker, and a poet of scurrility, who by giving too large a swinge to his own wit, and suffering his lust to have the full reins, fell (not without just desert) to the outrage and extremity that he denied God and his son Christ, and not only in word blasphemed the Trinity, but also (as it is credibly reported) wrote books against it, affirming our Savior to be but a deceiver, and Moses to be but a conjurer and seducer of the people, and the Holy Bible to be but vain and idle stories, and all religion but a device of policy.

But see what a hook the Lord put in the nostrils of this barking dog. It so fell out that in London streets as he purposed to stab one whom he owed a grudge unto with his dagger, the other party perceiving so avoided the stroke, that withal catching hold of his wrist, he stabbed his own dagger into his own head, in such sort that notwithstanding all the means of surgery that could be wrought, he shortly after died thereof. The manner of his death being so terrible (for he even cursed and blasphemed to his last gasp, and together with his breath an oath flew out of his mouth) that it was not only a manifest sign of God's judgment, but also an horrible and fearful terror to all that beheld him. But herein did the justice of God most notably appear, in that he compelled his own hand which had written those blasphemies to be the instrument to punish him, and that in his brain, which had devised the same.

I would to God (and I pray it from my heart) that all atheists in this realm, and in all the world beside, would by the remembrance and consideration of this example, either forsake their horrible impiety, or that they might in like manner come to destruction. And so that abominable sin which so flourisheth amongst men of greatest name might either be extinguished and rooted out, or at least smothered and kept under, that it durst not show it head any more in the world's eye.

(Sig. K5r-v)

The source of *Doctor Faustus*

Doctor Faustus has a single primary source, *The History of the Damnable Life and Deserved Death of Doctor John Faustus*, otherwise known as *The English Faust Book*. It is a translation, by an unknown 'P. F., Gent.,' of a work published in Germany in 1587. It gives an imaginative account of the life and death of Faustus, a real historical figure who died around 1539. The historical Faustus was an itinerant alchemist and astrologer, and various legends developed around his supposed necromancy and pact with the devil. These built on tales of magicians going all the way back to Simon Magus in the Biblical Acts of the Apostles, who in some later accounts is associated with Helen of Troy. The German and English *Faust Books* elaborated Faustus's adventures further. The first publication of *The English Faust Book* was in 1592, but Marlowe may have known an earlier version. In any event, it provides not only many of the key scenes of *Doctor Faustus* but much of the language of the play. Notably, it includes not only the heavily moralized stories of Faustus's pact with Mephistopheles and eventual damnation, but many of the adventures and comic episodes that make up the middle part of the play, in which Faustus appears as a trickster-hero.

From *The History of the Damnable Life and Deserved Death of Doctor John Faustus*, by P. F., Gent. (1592)

How Doctor Faustus began to practise in his devilish art, and how he conjured the devil, making him to appear and meet him on the morrow at his own house. Chap. 2

You have heard before, that all Faustus's mind was set to study the arts of necromancy and conjuration, the which exercise he followed day and night ... that in all the haste he put in practice to bring the devil before him. And taking his way to a thick wood near to Wittenberg ... he came into the same wood towards evening into a crossway, where he made with a wand a circle in the dust, and within that many more circles and characters: and thus he passed away the time, until it was nine or ten of the clock in the night, then began Doctor Faustus to call on Mephistopheles the spirit, and to charge him in the name of Beelzebub to appear there personally without any long stay: then presently the devil began so great a rumor in the wood, as if heaven and earth would have come together with wind, the trees bowing their tops to the ground. Then fell the devil to blare as if the whole wood had been full of lions, and suddenly about the circle ran the devil as if a thousand wagons had been running together on paved stones. After this at the four corners of the wood it thundered horribly, with such lightnings as if the whole world, to his seeming, had been on fire. Faustus all this while half amazed at the devil's so long tarrying, and doubting whether he were best to abide any more such horrible conjurings, thought to leave his circle and depart; whereupon the devil made him such music of all sorts, as if the nymphs themselves had been in place: whereat Faustus was revived and stood stoutly in his circle aspecting his purpose, and began again to conjure the spirit Mephistopheles in the name of the prince of devils to appear in his likeness: whereat suddenly over his head hanged hovering in the air a mighty dragon. Then calls Faustus again after his devilish manner, at which there was a monstrous cry in the wood, as if hell had been open, and all the tormented souls crying to God for mercy. Presently not three fathom above his head fell a flame in manner of a lightning, and changed itself into a globe: yet Faustus feared it not, but did persuade himself that the devil should give him his request before he would leave …. Faustus, vexed at the spirit's so long tarrying, used his charms with full purpose not to depart before he had his intent, and crying on Mephistopheles the spirit, suddenly the globe opened and sprang up in height of a man: so burning a time, in the end it converted to the shape of a fiery man. This pleasant beast ran about the circle a great while, and lastly appeared in the manner of a gray friar, asking Faustus what was his request. Faustus commanded that the next morning at twelve of the clock he should appear to him at his house; but the devil would in no wise grant. Faustus began again to conjure him in the name of Beelzebub, that he should fulfill his request: whereupon the spirit agreed, and so they departed each one his way. (*The English Faust Book: A Critical Edition*, 93–4)

How Doctor Faustus set his blood in a saucer on warm ashes and writ as followeth. Chap. 6

I Johannes Faustus, Doctor, do openly acknowledge with mine own hand, to the greater force and strengthening of this letter, that sithence I began to study and speculate the course and order of the elements, I have not found through the gift that is given me from above, any such learning and wisdom, that can bring me to my desires; and for that I find, that men are unable to instruct me any further in the matter, now have I Doctor John Faustus, unto the hellish prince of Orient and his messenger

Mephistopheles, given both body and soul, upon such condition, that they shall learn me, and fulfill my desire in all things, as they have promised and vowed unto me, with due obedience unto me, according unto the articles mentioned between us.

Further, I covenant and grant with them by these presents, that at the end of 24 years next ensuing the date of this present letter, they being expired, and I in the mean time, during the said years, be served of them at my will, they accomplishing my desires to the full in all points as we are agreed, that then I give them full power to do with me at their pleasure, to rule, to send, fetch or carry me or mine, be it either body, soul, flesh, blood or goods, into their habitation, be it wheresoever. And hereupon, I defy God and His Christ, all the host of heaven, and all living creatures that bear the shape of God, yea all that lives; and again I say it, and it shall be so. And to the more strengthening of this writing, I have written it with mine own hand and blood, being in perfect memory, and hereupon I subscribe to it with my name and title, calling all the infernal, middle and supreme powers to witness of this my letter and subscription.

John Faustus, approved in the elements, and the spiritual doctor.

(*The English Faust Book: A Critical Edition*, 98–9)

How Doctor Faustus deceived an Horse-courser. Chap. 34

In like manner he served an Horse-courser at a fair called Pheiffring, for Doctor Faustus through his cunning had gotten an excellent fair horse, whereupon he rid to the fair, where he had many chapmen that offered him money: lastly, he sold him for 40 dollars, willing him that bought him, that in any wise he should not ride him over any water, but the Horse-courser marveled with himself that Faustus bad him ride him over no water. 'But,' quoth he, 'I will prove,' and forthwith he rid him into the river. Presently the horse vanished from under him, and he sat on a bundle of straw, in so much that the man was almost drowned. The Horse-courser knew well where he lay that had sold him his horse, wherefore he went angerly to his inn, where he found Doctor Faustus fast asleep, and snorting on a bed, but the Horse-courser could no longer forbear him, took him by the leg and began to pull him off the bed, but he pulled him so, that he pulled his leg from his body, in so much that the Horse-courser fell down backwards in the place. Then began Doctor Faustus to cry with an open throat: 'He hath murdered me.' Hereat the Horse-courser was afraid, and gave the flight, thinking none other with himself, but that he had pulled his leg from his body; by this means Doctor Faustus kept his money.

(*The English Faust Book: A Critical Edition*, 153–4)

How Doctor Faustus played a merry jest with the Duke of Anholt in his Court. Chap. 39

Doctor Faustus on a time came to the Duke of Anholt, the which welcomed him very courteously; this was in the month of January, where sitting at the table, he perceived the Duchess to be with child, and forbearing himself until the meat was taken from the table, and that they brought in the banqueting dishes, said Doctor Faustus to the Duchess: 'Gracious lady, I have always heard, that the great bellied women do always long for some dainties. I beseech therefore Your Grace hide not your mind from me, but tell me what you desire to eat.' She answered him: 'Doctor Faustus, now truly I will not hide from you what my heart doth most desire, namely, that if it were now harvest, I would eat my belly full of ripe grapes, and other dainty fruit.' Doctor Faustus answered hereupon: 'Gracious Lady, this is a small thing for me to do, for I can do more than this.' Wherefore he took a plate, and made open one of the casements of the window, holding it forth, where incontinent he had his dish full of all manner of fruits, as red and white grapes, pears, and apples, the which came from out of strange countries. All these he presented the Duchess, saying: 'Madame, I pray you vouchsafe to taste of this dainty fruit, the which came from a far country, for there the summer is not yet ended.' The Duchess thanked Faustus highly, and she fell to her fruit with full appetite. The Duke of Anholt notwithstanding could not withhold to ask Faustus with what reason there were such young fruit to be had at that time of the year? Doctor Faustus told him: 'May it please your Grace to understand, that the year is divided into two circles over the whole world, that when with us it is winter, in the contrary circle it is notwithstanding summer, for in India and Saba there falleth or setteth the sun, so that it is so warm that they have twice a year fruit: and, gracious Lord, I have a swift spirit, the which can in the twinkling of an eye fulfill my desire in anything, wherefore I sent him into those countries, who hath brought this fruit as you see,' whereat the duke was in great admiration.

(The English Faust Book: A Critical Edition, 155–6)

How Doctor Faustus showed the fair Helena unto the Students upon the Sunday following. Chap. 45

The Sunday following came these students home to Doctor Faustus his own house, and brought their meat and drink with them: these men were right welcome guests unto Faustus, wherefore they all fell to drinking of wine smoothly: and being merry, they began some of them to talk of the beauty of women, and every one gave forth his verdict what he had seen and what he had heard. So one among the rest said: 'I never was so desirous of any thing in this world, as to have a sight (if it were possible) of fair Helena of Greece, for whom the worthy town of Troy was destroyed and razed down to the ground.' Therefore, sayeth he, that in all men's judgement she was more than commonly fair, because that when she was stolen away from her husband, there was for her recovery so great blood-shed.

Doctor Faustus answered: 'For that you are all my friends and are so desirous to see that famous pearl of Greece, fair Helena, the wife of King Menelaus and daughter of Tyndareus and Leda, sister to Castor and Pollux, who was the fairest lady in all Greece: I will therefore bring her into your presence personally, and in the same form of attire as she used to go when she was in her chiefest flower and pleasantest prime of youth. The like have I done for the Emperor Carolus Quintus: at his desire I showed him Alexander the Great, and his paramour. But,' said Doctor Faustus, 'I charge you all that upon your perils you speak not a word, nor rise up from the table so long as she is in your presence.' And so he went out of the Hall, returning presently again, after whom immediately followed the fair and beautiful Helena, whose beauty was such that the students were all amazed to see her, esteeming her rather to be a heavenly than an earthly creature. This lady appeared before them in a most sumptuous gown of purple velvet, richly imbrodered. Her hair hanged down loose as fair as the beaten gold, and of such length that it reached down to her hams; with amorous coal-black eyes, a sweet and pleasant round face, her lips red as a cherry, her cheeks of roseal colour, her mouth small, her neck as white as the swan, tall and slender of personage, and in sum, there was not one imperfect part in her. She looked round about her with a rolling hawk's eye, a smiling and wanton countenance, which near hand inflamed the hearts of the students but that they persuaded themselves she was a spirit, wherefore such fantasies passed away lightly with them: and thus fair Helena and Doctor Faustus went out again one with another. But the students at Doctor Faustus his entering again into the hall, requested of him to let them see her again the next day, for that they would bring with them a painter and so take her counterfeit, which he denied, affirming that he could not always raise up her spirit, but only at certain times. 'Yet,' said he, 'I will give you her counterfeit, which shall be always as good to you as if your selves should see the drawing thereof,' which they received according to his promise, but soon lost it again. The students departed from Faustus home every one to his house, but they were not able to sleep the whole night for thinking on the beauty of fair Helena. Wherefore a man may see that the devil blindeth and enflameth the heart with lust oftentimes, that men fall in love with harlots, nay, even with furies, which afterward cannot lightly be removed.

(*The English Faust Book: A Critical Edition*, 162–3)

An oration of Faustus to the Students. Chap. 63

My trusty and well-beloved friends, the cause why I have invited you into this place is this: forasmuch as you have known me this many years, in what manner of life I have lived, practising all manner of conjurations and wicked exercises, the which I have obtained through the help of the devil, into whose devilish fellowship they have brought me, the which use the like art and practise, urged by the detestable provocation of my flesh, my stiff-necked and rebellious will, with my filthy infernal thoughts, the which were ever before me, pricking me forward so earnestly that I must perforce have the consent of the devil to aid me in my desires. And to the end I might the better bring my purpose to pass, to have the devil's aid and furtherance, which I never have wanted in mine actions, I have promised unto him at the end and accomplishing of 24 years, both body and soul, to do therewith at his pleasure: and this day, this dismal day, those 24 years are fully expired, for night beginning, my hour-glass is at an end, the direful finishing whereof I carefully expect: for out of all doubt this night he will fetch me, to whom I have given my self in recompense of his service, both body and soul, and twice confirmed writings with my proper blood. Now have I called you my well-beloved lords, friends, brethren, and fellows, before that fatal hour, to take my friendly farewell, to the end that my departing may not hereafter be hidden from you, beseeching you herewith, courteous and loving lords and brethren, not to take in evil part any thing done by me, but with friendly commendations to salute all my friends and companions wheresoever: desiring both you and them, if ever I have trespassed against your minds in any thing, that you would all heartily forgive me: and as for those lewd practices the which this full 24 years I have followed, you shall hereafter find them in writing: and I beseech you let this my lamentable end to the residue of your lives be a sufficient warning, that you have God always before your eyes, praying unto Him that He would ever defend you from the temptation of the devil and all his false deceits, not falling altogether from God as I, wretched and ungodly damned creature, have done, having denied and defied baptism, the sacraments of Christ's body, God Himself, all heavenly powers and earthly men, yea, I have denied such a God that desireth not to have one lost. Neither let the evil fellowship of wicked companions mislead you as it hath done me. Visit earnestly and oft the Church, war and strive continually against the devil with a good and steadfast belief in God and Jesus Christ, and use your vocation in holiness. Lastly, to knit up my troubled oration, this is my friendly request, that you would to rest, and let nothing trouble you: also if you chance to hear any noise, or rumbling about the house, be not therewith afraid, for there shall no evil happen unto you: also I pray you arise not out of your beds. But above all things I entreat you, if you hereafter find my dead carcass, convey it unto the earth, for I die both a good and bad Christian; a good Christian, for that I am heartily sorry, and in my heart always pray for mercy, that my soul may be delivered: a bad Christian, for that I know the devil will have my body, and that would I willingly give him so that he would leave my soul in quiet: wherefore I pray you that you would depart to bed, and so I wish you a quiet night which unto me notwithstanding will be horrible and fearful.

This oration or declaration was made by Doctor Faustus, and that with a hearty and resolute mind, to the end he might not discomfort them: but the students wondered greatly thereat, that he was so blinded, for knavery, conjuration and such like foolish things, to give his body and soul unto the devil: for they loved him entirely, and never suspected any such thing before he had opened his mind to them: wherefore one of them said unto him: 'Ah, friend Faustus, what have you done to conceal this matter so long from us? We would by the help of good divines, and the grace of God, have brought you out of this net and have torn you out of the bondage and chains of Satan, whereas now we fear it is too late, to the utter ruin of your body and soul.' Doctor Faustus answered: 'I durst never do it, although I often minded to settle my self unto godly people, to desire counsel and help, as once mine old neighbour counselled me, that I should follow his learning, and leave all my conjurations. Yet when I was minded to amend, and to follow that good man's counsel, then came the devil and would have had me away, as this night he is like to do, and said, so soon as I turned again to God, he would dispatch me altogether. Thus, even thus, (good gentlemen, and my dear friends) was I enthralled in that satanical band, all good desires drowned, all piety banished, all purpose of amendment utterly exiled, by the tyrannous threatenings of my deadly enemy.' But when the students heard his words, they gave him counsel to do naught else but call upon God, desiring Him for the love of His sweet son Jesus Christ's sake, to have mercy upon him, teaching him this form of prayer: O God be merciful unto me, poor and miserable sinner, and enter not into judgement with me, for no flesh is able to stand before thee. Although, O Lord, I must leave my sinful body unto the devil, being by him deluded, yet thou in mercy mayest preserve my soul.

This they repeated unto him, yet it could take no hold, but even as Cain he also said his sins were greater than God was able to forgive; for all his thought was on his writing: he meant he had made it too filthy in writing it with his own blood. The students and the other that were there, when they had prayed for him, they wept, and so went forth, but Faustus tarried in the hall: and when the gentlemen were laid in bed, none of them could sleep, for that they attended to hear if they might be privy of his end. It happened between twelve and one o'clock at midnight, there blew a mighty storm of wind against the house as though it would have blown the foundation thereof out of his place. Hereupon the students began to fear and got out of their beds, comforting one another, but they would not stir out of the chamber: and the host of the house ran out of doors, thinking the house would fall. The students lay near unto that hall wherein Doctor Faustus lay, and they heard a mighty noise and hissing as if the hall had been full of snakes and adders: with that the hall door flew open wherein Doctor Faustus was, then he began to cry for help, saying: 'Murder, murder!' but it came forth with half a voice hollowly: shortly after they heard him no more. But when it was day, the students, that had taken no rest that night, arose and went into the hall in the which they left Doctor Faustus, where notwithstanding they found no Faustus, but all the hall lay besprinkled with blood, his brains cleaving to the wall: for the devil had beaten him from one wall against another, in one corner lay his eyes, in another his teeth, a pitiful and fearful sight to behold. Then began the students to bewail and weep for him, and sought for his body in many places: lastly they came into the yard where they found his body lying on the horse dung, most monstrously torn, and fearful to behold, for his head and all his joints were dashed in pieces.

The forenamed students and masters that were at his death, have obtained so much that they buried him in the village where he was so grievously tormented. After the which, they returned to Wittenberg, and coming into the house of Faustus, they found the servant of Faustus very sad, unto whom they opened all the matter, who took it exceeding heavily. There found they also this history of Doctor Faustus, noted and of him written as is before declared, all save only his end, the which was after by the students thereto annexed: further, what his servant had noted thereof, was made in another book. And you have heard that he held by him in his life the spirit of fair Helena, the which had by him one son, the which he named Justus Faustus: even the same day of his death they vanished away, both mother and son. The house before was so dark that scarce anybody could abide therein. The same night Doctor Faustus appeared unto his servant lively, and showed unto him many secret things the which he had done and hidden in his lifetime. Likewise there were certain which saw Doctor Faustus look out of the window by night as they passed by the house.

And thus ended the whole history of Doctor Faustus his conjuration and other acts that he did in his life; out of the which example every Christian may learn, but chiefly the stiff-necked and high-minded may thereby learn to fear God and to be careful of their vocation, and to be at defiance with all devilish works, as God hath most precisely forbidden, to the end we should not invite the devil as a guest, nor give him place as that wicked Faustus hath done: for here we have a fearful example of his writing, promise and end, that we may remember him: that we go not astray, but take God always before our eyes, to call alone upon Him, and to honour Him all the days of our life, with heart and hearty prayer, and with all our strength and soul to glorify His holy name, defying the devil and all his works, to the end we may remain with Christ in all endless joy: Amen, amen, that wish I unto every Christian heart, and God's name to be glorified. Amen. FINIS.

(The English Faust Book: A Critical Edition, 177–81)

Renaissance magic

Doctor Faustus draws on traditions of early modern magic associated not only with the historical Faustus himself but with Cornelius Agrippa, who is mentioned in the first scene as an exemplar of necromantic cunning. Agrippa (1486–1535), a more or less exact contemporary of the historical Faustus, was, like him, a German doctor and alchemist, though he moved in higher circles, eventually becoming a physician to the French court. Among his published writings is *Of Occult Philosophy*, which defends magic from charges of heresy and attempts to effect a Neoplatonic synthesis between science, magic, and faith.

Of Occult Philosophy, by Cornelius Agrippa (1531)

To the reader

I do not doubt but the title of our *Book of Occult Philosophy*, or *of Magic*, may by the rarity of it allure many to read it, amongst which, some of a crazy judgment and some that are perverse will come to hear what I can say, who, by their rash ignorance may take the name of "magic" in the worse sense, and though scarce having seen the title, cry out that I teach forbidden arts, sow the seed of heresies, offend pious ears, and scandalize excellent wits; that I am a sorcerer, and superstitious and devilish, [and] indeed am a magician. To whom I answer, that a magician doth not amongst learned men signify a sorcerer, or one that is superstitious or devilish, but a wise man, a priest, a prophet; and that the Sybils were magicianesses, and therefore prophesied most clearly of Christ; and that Magicians, as wise men, by the wonderful secrets of the world, knew Christ, the author of the world, to be born, and came first of all to worship him; and that the name of "magic" was received by philosophers, commended by divines, and not unacceptable to the Gospel. I believe that the supercilious censors will object against the Sybils, holy magicians, and the Gospel itself sooner then receive the name of "magic" into favour; so conscientious are they, that neither Apollo, nor all the muses, nor an angel from heaven can redeem me from their curse. Whom therefore I advise, that they read not our writings, nor understand them, nor remember them. For they are pernicious, and full of poison; the gate of Acheron is in this book. It speaks stones, let them take heed that it beat not out their brains. But you that come without prejudice to read it, if you have so much discretion of prudence, as bees have in gathering honey, read securely, and believe that you shall receive no little profit, and much pleasure; but if you shall find any things that may not please you, let them alone and make no use of them, for I do not approve of them, but declare them to you; but do not refuse other things, for they that look into the books of physicians do, together with antidotes and medicines, read also poisons. I confess that magic itself teacheth many superfluous things, and curious prodigies for ostentation. Leave them as empty things, yet be not ignorant of their causes. But those things which are for the profit of man, for the turning away of evil events, for the destroying of sorceries, for the curing of diseases, for the exterminating of phantasms, for the preserving of life, honour, or fortune, may be done without offense to God, or injury to religion, because they are, as profitable, so necessary...

(*Christopher Marlowe: Doctor Faustus, 227–8*)

Protestant theology: predestination and reprobation

Elizabethan Protestants believed that certain souls were elected, or predestined for salvation, by God, and that others were inevitably doomed to damnation. This argument follows logically from the notion of God's omniscience and foreknowledge, but it seems to take away any possibility of agency from the individual human, who is bound by his or her sinful nature and God's predestination. The influential Swiss Protestant thinker John Calvin argued that the reprobate, those destined to damnation, would necessarily be immune to grace. The notion of God's 'hardening the heart' of the reprobate sinner, discussed here by Calvin, is very relevant to the question of Faustus's spiritual condition. At one point Faustus declares, 'My heart's so hardened I cannot repent' (A. 2.3). The following excerpt from one of Calvin's most influential works suggests one way an Elizabethan audience might have understood Faustus's inability to repent.

From John Calvin's *Institutes of Christian Religion* (trans. Thomas Norton, 1561). Book 2, Chapter 4, Paragraph 3

It is oftentimes said that God blindeth and hardeneth the reprobate, that he turneth, boweth, and moveth their hearts, as I have elsewhere taught more at large. But of what manner that is, it is never expressed, if we flee to free foreknowledge or sufferance. Therefore we answer that it is done after two manners. For first, whereas when his light is taken away, there remaineth nothing but darkness and blindness, whereas when his spirit is taken away, our hearts wax hard and become stones, whereas when his direction ceaseth, they are wrestled into crookedness. It is well said that he doth blind, harden, and bow them from whom he taketh away the power to see, obey and do rightly. The second manner, which cometh near to the property of the words, is that for the executing of his judgments by Satan, the minister of his wrath, he both appointeth their purposes to what end it pleaseth him, and stirreth up their wills and strengtheneth their endeavours. So when Moses rehearseth that King Sehon did not give passage to the people because God had hardened his spirit and made his heart obstinate, he by and by adjoineth the end of his purpose: that he might (sayeth he) give him unto our hands. Therefore because it was God's will to have him destroyed, the making of his heart obstinate was God's preparation for his destruction.

4 Key Performances and Productions

Although *Doctor Faustus* was one of the most popular plays of the early modern stage, it can hardly be said to have been performed at all from the closing of the theatres in 1642 until the eve of the twentieth century. When Puritan authorities put an end to dramatic performances in England in the run-up to the civil war, they made an irrevocable break in the traditions of the Renaissance theatre. There was no drama performed publicly in England for a generation, until the Restoration of Charles II. The theatres that opened in 1660 were very different from those of the early modern period, with female actors and perspective scenery only the most obvious changes. Tastes had changed and memories had faded during the 18 years when there was no theatre in London. Marlowe's star had waned, and his most famous play, which had remained popular for decades after his death, was now mainly a vehicle for music, dance, and comedy, and would not be revived in its own right for more than 200 years.

Seventeenth to nineteenth centuries

Though Thomas Betterton, the greatest Restoration actor, played Faustus in 1662, the play was not to the taste of the times; Samuel Pepys found it 'so wretchedly and poorly done that we were sick of it' (*Diary*, 20 May 1662). The version Pepys saw was presumably that published in 1663; the last publication of a largely Marlovian text of the play until 1814. It follows the B-text reasonably closely, though with some excisions of explicitly religious material, changes that may date from the period of Puritan ascendancy. There is one notable change that was presumably made after the Restoration, when anti-Catholic attitudes had somewhat eased under Charles II. In place of the scene with the Pope, Betterton's Faustus appeared at the court of the Turkish Sultan Solomaine, in a scene partly based on an episode from Marlowe's *The Jew of Malta*, and perhaps influenced by William Davenant's popular opera *The Siege of Rhodes*. The scene takes place in Babylon, where the Ottomans are celebrating their recent victory over Malta, achieved with the help of Mephistopheles and a Jew based on Marlowe's Barabas. The invisible Faustus mocks bashaws instead of cardinals, steals a kiss from Solomaine's Empress, and, with Mephistopheles' help, confounds the Sultan's conjurer. Interestingly, the kissing of the Empress echoes an episode in *The English Faust Book* not used by Marlowe, in which Faustus seduces the Turk's wives while disguised as Mahomet. Perhaps the adaptor had access to Marlowe's source, or, just possibly, to a lost Marlovian version of the play which included the Turkish episode (the distinguished critic William Empson, in his final, uncompleted work, argued for the existence of such a version).

Subsequent adaptors molded the play to contemporary fashions by adding comic episodes with *commedia* clowns and inserting liberal amounts of music, dance, and magic – developing the movement toward spectacle already present in the B-text. William Mountfort, who had played Mephistopheles to Betterton's Faustus, extended this trend with his *Life and Death of Doctor Faustus, Made into a Farce*, published in 1697. Mountfort uses some of Marlowe's original text, but it is much compressed to allow for 'the Humours of Harlequin and Scaramouche' advertised on the title page. For instance, Faustus's first speech, with which the play begins, is reduced from Marlowe's 65 lines to the following:

> Settle thy study, Faustus, and begin
> To sound the depth of that thou wilt profess.
> These metaphysics of magicians,
> And necromantic books are heavenly.
> Lines, circles, letters, characters,
> Ay, these are those that Faustus most desires;
> A sound magician is a demi-god:
> Here tire my brains to get a deity. (p. 1)

The Good and Bad Angels immediately appear, followed by Mephistopheles; but within 20 lines they have been interrupted by cries from Scaramouche, who runs in shouting, 'O I beseech you, conjure no more, for I am frighted into a Diabetes already!' (p. 2).

Scaramouche combines elements of Wagner and Robin. Harlequin, who soon joins him, roughly corresponds to Rafe or Dick. Their scenes, built upon the comic episodes in Marlowe's *Faustus* but considerably expanded, take up about a third of this quite short play. The parts featuring Faustus and Mephistopheles largely use a much-abbreviated Marlovian text, and are not inherently farcical, except where Marlowe is (as in the Horse-courser sequence). They include versions of the blood contract, the Helen episode, the warnings of the Old Man, the Emperor and Benvolio, and the antics with Faustus's false head and false leg. Most of these are much curtailed. One episode that is expanded is that of the Seven Deadly Sins, who are given augmented pedigrees that arguably improve on those in the A- and B-texts. Gluttony, for instance, says he was 'begot by a plowman on a washerwoman, who devoured a cheddar cheese in two hours'; Sloth was 'begotten at church by a sleepy judge upon a costermonger's wife, in the middle of a long sermon' (p. 11). The play ends with Faustus dragged to hell, and his torn limbs discovered; however, the final stage directions read: '*Scene changes to Hell. Faustus' Limbs come together. A Dance, and Song*' (p. 26). Exactly how this was achieved is hard to visualize, but it no doubt made an entertaining conclusion for audiences in the period.

In the next known versions, from the early eighteenth century, Marlowe's text is gone entirely. Apparently, in the 1720s, there was a kind of battle of the Faustuses, as the two licensed theatres both staged farcical entertainments based on the conjurer. The Theatre Royal Drury Lane presented *Harlequin Doctor Faustus*, which featured Mr Shaw as Faustus and Mr Thurmond as Mephistopheles, but also included the three students Scaramouch, Punch, and Pierot, as well as such characters as the Usurer, the Bawd, the Courtesan, the Salesman, his Wife, and the Landlady, plus a whole list of 'Heathen Deities.' The published version includes only *commedia*-style scenarios of the interactions, which mainly feature conjuring tricks whereby Faustus defrauds the various citizens, somewhat in the spirit of the Horse-courser leg-episode. The other Theatre Royal at Lincoln's Inn Fields presented a rival entertainment called *The Necromancer*. For this at least some text is preserved, though not a word of it is by Marlowe. Faustus is discovered reading at a table, and the Good and Bad Spirits give their contrary advice. Helen appears, summoned by the Bad Spirit, and Faustus is struck by her beauty, at which 'the Infernal Spirit interposes,' saying, 'Hold; --and the Terms of Pleasure know;/ This contract sign, thy Faith to bind,/ Then revel in Delight at large,/ And give a loose to joy' (p. 8). Faustus signs, of course, though he is deprived of bliss by the appearance of the Phantom of Envy. The remaining scenes show Faustus demonstrating his magic by conjuring Hero and Leander, and Faustus raising spirits for an 'Antick Dance.'

> *As they are performing, a Clock strikes, the Doctor is seiz'd, hurried away by Spirits, and devour'd by the Monster, which immediately takes Flight; and while it is disappearing, Spirits vanish, and other Daemons rejoice in the following Words:*
>
> Now triumph Hell, and Fiends be gay,
> The Sorc'rer is become our Prey. (p. 15)

The anonymous editor of the two "entertainments" writes that he has collected them for posterity, 'that they may have the pleasure of seeing, in print at least, the wonderful tricks and powerful art of the so much talked of Faustus, as performed at both theatres' (*An Exact Description of the Two Fam'd Entertainments of Harlequin Doctor Faustus*, Preface). It seems that 'wonderful tricks,' together with dancing and comedy, were the principal attractions of the play for the period.

After this, Marlowe's *Faustus* was lost to the stage for the next century and a half. In the meantime Goethe drew on the same story to create his own masterpiece of magic, philosophy, and spiritual conflict. Goethe's *Faust* owes little to Marlowe's, though the German writer is said to have known the work of his English predecessor. The English lawyer and diarist Henry Crabb Robertson, visiting Weimar in 1818, reported that Goethe praised Marlowe's play, exclaiming 'How greatly is it all planned!' (*Diary*, Vol. 2, 434). Goethe's work, and its operatic adaptations by Gounod and Boito, became well known in England, and many English writers read and commented on Marlowe's work after it was republished in the 1814 collection *Old English Plays*. Critics such as William Hazlitt, perhaps influenced by Goethe, embraced Marlowe's *Faustus* as a romantic hero, a Prometheus martyred through his humanist quest for knowledge. And as early as 1866, the critic Henry Morley, noting the popularity of the story, suggested that 'Now that Faust is in the ascendant, it might even be said that freedom of omission in the comic scenes, with elsewhere two or three skillful modifications, would give to our stage in Marlowe's Faustus a grand part for a good actor' (*Examiner* 1866). But the play remained off the stage. When Henry Irving, the greatest Victorian actor, played Mephistopheles in 1885, it was in a rewritten version of Goethe's text by the Irish dramatist W. G. Wills. The text hardly mattered, however, as spectacle was the focus of the production, with the new technology of calcium arc lights and electric spark machines contributing to the diablerie. The expensive production proved to be one of Irving's most profitable, but the literati scorned it: Henry James wrote that 'special precautions should be taken against the accessories seeming a more important part of the business than the action' (*The Century*). Asked whether he had seen the production, W. S. Gilbert sniffed, 'I go to pantomime only at Christmas' (*A Strange Eventful History*, 174).

English Stage Society (William Poel), 1896

It remained for William Poel, the great proselyte for the Elizabethan Revival, to bring Marlowe's text back before the English theatre-going public. The Victorian theatre, with its dominant actor-managers, large theatres, and advanced scenic technology, performed Shakespeare in drastically cut and altered texts. Poel was determined to get back to a more Elizabethan style of performance, as he understood it, and was also interested in exploring the works of Shakespeare's lesser-known contemporaries. Accordingly, he founded the Elizabethan Stage Society; their third production, on 2 July 1896, was of *Doctor Faustus*. There were of course no Renaissance-style theatres in existence, so he erected something approximating an Elizabethan stage in St George's Hall (though the audience viewed the performance wholly from the front). Poel restaged the production at the Royal Court in 1904, setting his stage within the theatre's proscenium, and then took the production on tour around Great Britain.

Poel divided the play into three acts, using the 1604 version as his primary text. The first act ended with the Seven Deadly Sins; the second contained the Pope, Emperor, and Vanholt scenes and concluded with Faustus's reflections on his impending end; and the third contained Faustus's encounters with the scholars, Helen of Troy, and the Old Man, together with his last speech and the closing chorus. Poel noted in his program that 'There is no justification for reviving with historical accuracy the middle part of the play, which is not Marlowe's.' Accordingly, he felt free to conclude the middle section with a masque presented to the Duke and Duchess of Vanholt in which several of the Deadly Sins joined with skeletons and imps in a Dance of Death, which is featured in the one surviving photograph of the production.

Poel's stage had a second-level, curtained discovery space, and doors at the back. His set and staging were based on his understanding of period sources such as the contract for the Fortune theatre, the sketch of the Swan stage, and accounts of the pageant wagons of the medieval mystery plays. Conjuration scenes drew on Reginald Scot's sixteenth-century text *The Discoverie of Witchcraft*. The stagecraft had a formalized spatial language, with comic scenes played downstage before the curtain, localized scenes in the discovery space, the Good Angel always entering from stage right, a hell-mouth at the back, and Lucifer watching from the balcony. Descriptions and images suggest that the costuming was elaborate and drew heavily on Poel's knowledge of art history. The angels were designed after Botticelli, devils after the façade of Notre Dame Cathedral. Faustus himself wore 'a surplice/With a cross upon his breast,' as in the 1609 reference in Rowlands' *Knave of Clubs*. For conjuring, he added a stole with alchemical symbols; later he adopted a rich fur-lined gown. Mephistopheles, when dressed as a friar, wore a gray gown with a cowl that completely concealed his face, and that according to several reports contained an incandescent light bulb, a special effect that seems at odds with Poel's impulse toward authenticity.

One celebrated moment was the appearance of Helen of Troy. As Robert Speaight described it: 'The actress was given a long walk upstage, with her face three-quarters turned away from the audience; all her beauty could be read in the rapt expression on Faustus' face, and there was no risk of rhetoric being contradicted by reality' (*William Poel*, 115). Poel's Victorianism came through in the interaction of Helen with Faustus: she kissed his forehead and she kissed his hand; later in the 1904 revival he was permitted a chaste kiss on her cheek.

The production was hampered, many critics felt, by Poel's idiosyncratic ideas about verse-speaking. He had his actors chant in a system of what he called 'tuned tones,' resulting in a 'slow, woebegone, sepulchral delivery,' according to the *Daily Telegraph* (3 July 1896). Nonetheless, many felt that the production's antiquarian methods provided insights, though their characterization of the Elizabethan theatre was somewhat condescending. The critic of the *Manchester Guardian*, who saw the play on tour, noted that:

> one was helped to feel the tremendous difference between the two forms of stage upon the drama that used them. The platform stage obviously made naturalism in acting impossible and declamation essential... On such a stage Elizabethan drama had to be a drama of harangues, as on our own stage – an illusive hole in the wall – drama is almost bound over to be realistic. (8 November 1904)

The playwright and critic George Bernard Shaw, who condemned Marlowe as 'the true Elizabethan blank-verse beast, itching to frighten other people with the superstitious terrors and cruelties in which he does not himself believe,' nonetheless declared that 'Kit Marlowe... did not bore me at St. George's Hall as he has always bored me when I have tried to read him without skipping.' (*Saturday Review* 11 July 1896). Writing in the same issue, Shaw praised Poel's approach to the staging:

> The more I see of these performances by the Elizabethan Stage Society, the more I am convinced that their method of presenting an Elizabethan play is not only the right method for that particular sort of play, but that any play performed on a platform stage amidst the audience gets closer home to its hearers than when it is presented as a picture framed by a proscenium.

Poel's success with the production brought Marlowe's text back into the dramatic repertory. The actor-managers Herbert Beerbohm-Tree and Ben Greet performed it in London and New York respectively in 1908 and 1910; the experimental director Nugent Monck produced it in Canterbury in 1929; and there were productions at various universities, including Marlowe's own alma mater, Cambridge, where the Marlowe Dramatic Society was founded in 1908.

Federal Theatre Project (Orson Welles), 1937

One of the most notable productions of *Doctor Faustus* in US history was that given by the Federal Theatre Project, part of President Franklin Roosevelt's 'New Deal' effort to provide work for the

Depression-era unemployed (in this case, theatre-workers). Producer John Houseman and the young actor-director Orson Welles, who had previously collaborated on a Haitian-set *Macbeth*, staged Faustus for a 5-month run at the Maxine Elliott Theatre on New York's Broadway. The 21-year-old Welles, a prodigiously talented auteur who would make his mark in film 4 years later with *Citizen Kane*, was the primary creative force behind the production. As well as directing and playing the lead, he designed the sets and the costumes, which were inspired by Holbein's woodcut series *The Dance of Death*. The production was full of innovations in stagecraft and lighting; Brooks Atkinson, in the *New York Times*, said it went 'a long way toward revolutionizing the staging of Elizabethan plays' (9 January 1937).

The production used a bare stage with a sharply angled trapezoidal thrust extending out over the first several rows; Houseman believed it to be the first breach of the proscenium in a Broadway playhouse. There was no visible set; the space was carved up by shafts and curtains of light, provided by the newly developed ellipsoidal instruments and orchestrated by designer Abe Feder. The 63 light cues worked in tandem with three cylindrical drapes of black velvet to allow for startling appearances and disappearances. 'Orson was always, at heart, a magician,' wrote Houseman. 'His production of Marlowe's tragedy was designed and executed as a magic show' (*Run-through*, 233). Welles also made use of trap-doors, especially for the Seven Deadly Sins, which were grotesque puppets, 'lewd and nauseating, flopping about in the theatre box or at the feet of Faustus,' according to FTP director Hallie Flanagan (*Arena*, 187).

Welles viewed the Elizabethan theatre as fast-paced, fluid, and accessible, and was keen to recreate those qualities in his production. He used the A-text, cut heavily to run just over an hour. Faustus's opening speech was much abbreviated, moving the play quickly along to the conjuring of Mephistopheles. He was first presented by two giant terrifying eyes, suspended in the darkness, then in the person of Jack Carter, an African–American actor who had been the lead in the voodoo *Macbeth*. Carter was a coolly dignified Mephistopheles, tall and imposing, his gleaming bald head emerging from the cowl of his friar's gown. He had a compelling chemistry with Welles, as Houseman describes it:

> Their presence on the stage together was unforgettable: both were around
> six foot four, both men of abnormal strength capable of sudden furious

violence. Yet their scenes together were played with restraint, verging on tenderness, in which temptation and damnation were treated as acts of love. (*Run-through*, 236)

There was a strong element of robust comedy in the production. Welles included the encounter of Wagner and the Clown, who was played by an old vaudevillian named Harry McKee with cap, motley, and bauble; Stark Young declared him 'the best clown I have seen in Elizabethan revivals' (*New Republic* 17 February 1937). Welles also kept the first two Robin/Rafe scenes, combined into a single farcical sequence. The hijinks at the Papal court were a highlight of the production, using the inventive lighting to comic effect. As the procession of cardinals and friars carried the banquet ceremonially across the stage, 'a suckling pig was seen to rise from its golden dish, fly straight up to a height of twelve feet, execute a few steps of an obscene dance, then melt into thin air' – a process repeated with a haunch of beef, two chickens, and a pudding (*Run-through*, 234). The effect was achieved by black-clad dancers, invisible to the audience behind the curtain of light, plucking the properties aloft with flexible rods like fishing poles.

After the Pope's scene, however, the production turned immediately serious, cutting to Faustus's conjuring of Helen within 50 lines. Helen was an eerie figure, beautiful but remote in a pale mask. She appeared in a column of light at the back of the stage while Welles, in another on the apron, spoke the famous monologue out to the audience. Welles's Faustus was a haunted and driven man, richly clad but gauntly made-up, sweating with appetite and desperation. Houseman felt that:

> the legend of the man who sells his soul to the devil in exchange for knowledge and power and who must finally pay for his brief triumph with the agonies of eternal damnation was uncomfortably close to the shape of Welles' own personal myth. There were moments when Faustus seemed to be expressing, through Marlowe's words, some of Orson's own personal agony and private terror. (*Run-through*, 235)

As was the case with Richard Burton some years later, Welles brought his blazing talent and volatile personality to a role whose trajectory came to be identified with his own. *The Oxford Companion to the American Theatre* ends its entry on Welles with words that could be applied to Faustus: he was 'an example of one who either burnt himself out early or wasted his talents on futile efforts.' (p. 655). Welles's *Faustus* remains a landmark in the American theatre; seen by some 80,000 spectators, it is still the most successful production of the play on the Broadway stage. Years later, Welles staged his own free adaptation of the Faustus story, *Time Runs*, in Paris in 1950. Welles again played Faustus, with the Irish actor Hilton Edwards as Mephistopheles, the singer Eartha Kitt as Helen of Troy, and music by Duke Ellington.

Laboratory Theatre, Poland (Jerzy Grotowski), 1963

Doctor Faustus has had a limited production history outside the English-speaking world; much of that has been in central Europe, the source of the Faust legend. There is evidence of early productions in Graz, Austria (1608) and Dresden, Germany (1626) by the 'English Comedians', touring actors who brought the Elizabethan repertory to the continent. Goethe's version of the story held the stage in the eighteenth and nineteenth centuries, but in the early twentieth century, Marlowe's play was produced in translation in Heidelberg, Frankfurt, Hamburg, and other German cities, and it is now part of the international repertoire.

The revolutionary Polish director Jerzy Grotowski used Marlowe's *Faustus* as the basis for one of his most celebrated experimental productions at his Laboratory Theatre in Opole, Poland in 1963. Grotowski wanted to reduce theatre down to its most essential elements, stripping away scenery, lighting, music, and even the physical barriers between actors and audience. *Doctor Faustus* took place in a long, low room, some 40 by 15 feet. It used no props and simple costumes in white, black, and brown, combining religious habits with plain modern clothes. The 60 spectators sat at two long refectory tables, as in a monastery. A third, smaller table crossed them at one end. Most of the action took place on top of the tables in the midst of the audience. The whole play was presented as Faustus's last supper in the hour before his damnation.

Grotowski's production was steeped in religious ritual and iconography. Though a professed non-believer himself, Grotowski infused his theatrical practice with spiritual intensity and ascetic self-sacrifice. He interpreted Faustus as an anti-religious saint, a martyr in defiance of God. The production notes published in *Tulane Drama Review*, translated by Richard Schechner, declare:

> Faustus is a saint and his saintliness shows itself as an absolute desire
> for pure truth. If the saint is to become one with his sainthood, he must
> rebel against God, creator of the world, because the laws of the world are
> traps contradicting morality and truth. (*Tulane Drama Review*, 8:4 (Summer
> 1964), 121)

This anti-authoritarian interpretation of the play reflected both the general zeitgeist of the 1960s and Poland's painful history, as well as Grotowski's personal preoccupations.

Grotowski used Marlowe's B-text, translated into Polish, with extensive cuts and rearrangements. The production began with Faustus welcoming his guests, the audience, in a scene adapted from the meeting with the scholars in 5.2. With his arms outspread like Jesus on the Cross, he 'confesses as sins his studies and exalts as a virtue his act with the devil,' according to the 'textual montage' prepared by Grotowski and his assistant Eugenio Barba. At this point, the play shifted into a flashback, beginning with Faustus's opening monologue.

The production used few actors. Faustus was Zbigniew Cynkutis, a fair young man in white robes; Grotowski felt that his 'psychophysical characteristics' resembled traditional representations of St Sebastian. Mephistopheles was played by two actors, a man and a woman, dressed in black; they also played the Good and Evil Angels, the Seven Deadly Sins, and even the dragons who fly Faustus to Rome. The lines of the various low comic characters were spoken by two actors in modern costume seated among the audience. The most celebrated Grotowski actor, Ryszard Cieslak (who went on to play the lead in *The Constant Prince*), played Wagner, Valdes, the Pope, and Benvolio. As the last of these, he flew into a rage against Faustus and tore the tops from the trestle tables, physically dismantling the set.

The production emphasized the physicality of the actors, honed through Grotowski's rigorous training. There were many memorable moments, sometimes contradicting the text. While preparing to sign his contract with the Devil, Faustus endured a frenzied self-mortification and cleansing baptism, as the actors of Mephistopheles held him down in the 'river' between the two tables. The book containing the secrets of nature was the body of the devil-bride, which Faustus caressed and examined as he spoke of gaining knowledge of the heavens and earth. After Helen made love to Faustus, she gave birth to a baby, and then became the needy and demanding infant.

Grotowski made Faustus's final monologue a confrontation between Faustus and God. While using Marlowe's text, the actor made it clear that Faustus was exposing God's cruelty and indifference, calling the audience to witness the failure of the promises of salvation. Grotowski conceived of Faustus's death and damnation as his 'Passion'; he was carried off by the male Mephistopheles with his arms trailing behind him like the crucified Christ, while the female Mephistopheles followed as the *mater dolorosa*. Grotowski's ending was ambiguous in its presentation of the martyred Faustus, but unequivocal in its condemnation of the authoritarian God. The textual montage concludes with this account of Faustus's final exit:

> From the saint's mouth come raucous cries; these inarticulate sounds are not human. Faustus is no longer a man, but a panting animal, an unclaimed, once-human wreck moaning without dignity. The saint against God has attained his 'summit,' he has lived God's cruelty. He is the victor – morally. But he has paid the full price of that victory: eternal martyrdom in hell where all is taken from him, even his dignity. (*Towards a Poor Theatre*, 86–7)

The production established Grotowski's international reputation after it was seen by a number of Western critics attending a Warsaw theatre conference. It also anticipated some of the more experimental and exploratory productions of *Doctor Faustus* that would emerge decades later, including the RSC production of 1989 and the Old Vic production of 2002.

Oxford Playhouse (Nevill Coghill), 1966

The place of *Doctor Faustus* in the English literary canon meant that it was performed frequently at universities, even while it was seldom revived on the commercial stage. One of the most famous productions of *Doctor Faustus* in the twentieth century was given at the Oxford Playhouse in 1966, directed by Professor Nevill Coghill, with

Richard Burton and Elizabeth Taylor. Coghill, a driving force in the University's theatrical culture for decades, had met Burton when the latter came to Oxford in 1944 on an RAF training course and played Angelo in Coghill's *Measure for Measure*. After Burton achieved international celebrity, he returned to Oxford to play Faustus for Coghill, with his even-more-famous wife as Helen of Troy. The rest of the cast were students; the production was a benefit for Oxford student theatre and was Coghill's farewell production as a director.

Burton emphasized the less exalted aspects of Faustus's personality, his relish of childish pranks and sensual pleasures. Stocky, stolid, and bespectacled, he was an undistinguished figure who only rose to tragic heights in the final scenes. When he signed his soul over to Lucifer, he 'might have been signing a lease in a solicitor's ill-lit office,' W. A. Darlington complained in the *Telegraph* (15 February 1966). Burton's command of the lines was imperfect and his delivery was mainly conversational, with odd midline pauses that broke the rhythms of Marlowe's verse. Some critics thought he might have been keeping his performance low-key for the sake of his student colleagues, of whom Andreas Teuber, as Mephistopheles, was considered the most successful. The *Times* severely declared that 'Mr. Burton seemed to be walking through the part and his contributions to the stiff high-jinks in the Vatican are almost as embarrassing as those of the undergraduate actors' (15 February 1966). The comic scenes drew little praise, though the Seven Deadly Sins, played with giant papier-mâché carnival heads, made an impression. There was widespread condemnation of the horror movie-style Wurlitzer organ music, and a sense that the production overreached itself, with 'leaden pauses as characters encumbered with wings and unwieldy headdresses make long trudging exits' (*Times*).

Most critics agreed that Burton's final scenes were his best. Harold Hobson described Burton 'in an ecstasy of poetry, at first drunk with admiration as the marvelous beauty of Miss Taylor incarnates Troy's miraculous destroyer, and then electric in agony as he sees Christ's blood streaming in the firmament outside the reach of his imploring hand' (*Sunday Times* 20 February 1966). J. C. Trewin allowed only that 'no Faustus of intelligence could fail in that last hour of torment expressed in 60 lines, and intensified at Oxford by accelerating drumbeats that might have been the ticking of a clock or the thudding of a man's heart' (*Illustrated London News* 26 February

1966). Yet Trewin felt that Burton 'sketched a diagram of the part ...
he did not fill it out.'

While most critics damned the production, the appeal of the two
stars made it a great popular success, and it raised funds that contrib-
uted to the workshop space now known as the Burton–Taylor Studio.
Many who queued for hours for tickets were disappointed that
Taylor's role was such a brief and speechless cameo. Nonetheless, the
Oxford Mail critic enthused that 'the appearance of the one woman
whose beauty and fable can stand comparison with Marlowe's rolling
words inevitably lifts the atmosphere of the evening'; he also praised
Burton for 'the tempestuous magnificence with which he encompasses the torment of Faustus' end' (15 February 1966). Burton's rich
but rough-edged voice and somewhat dissipated persona were well
matched to a Faustus who frittered away his powers in self-indul-
gence. Many critics felt that Burton, potentially the greatest classical
actor of his generation, had wasted his gifts on poor films, drink, and
celebrity: the headline of Bernard Levin's review was 'What a dozen
years have done to Burton' (*Daily Mail* 15 February 1966). The parallel
with Faustus was one of which Burton himself was highly conscious.
'*Faustus* is the one play I don't have to do any work on,' he allegedly
told friends. 'I am Faustus' (*Burton*, 116).

Despite the production's poor reviews, the publicity around the
Burton–Taylor *Faustus* led to its being made into a film by Columbia
pictures, discussed in the next chapter.

RSC (Clifford Williams), 1968

Several of the most important productions of *Doctor Faustus* in the
twentieth century have been done in Stratford-Upon-Avon, the
birthplace of Marlowe's rival, Shakespeare, and home of the Royal
Shakespeare Company. The first Stratford production was by Walter
Hudd in 1946, with Robert Harris as Faustus and Hugh Griffith
as Mephistopheles (replaced in a 1947 revival by the young Paul
Scofield). It was notable chiefly for its towering unit set of balconies
and stairways, which allowed the action to flow fluidly from scene
to scene, although, as one critic noted, 'the amount of stair-climbing
involved must be tiresome to the players and is sometimes a little
tiresome to the audience' (*Manchester Guardian* 19 July 1946). For his

final speech, Faustus was placed not in his claustrophobic cell but on a high platform against the open sky, a choice that divided reviewers. J. C. Trewin felt the moment conveyed 'much of the man's last anguish, unutterable loneliness and despair', (*Observer* 14 July 1946), while the *Times* critic found it a showy trick: 'Mr. Hudd places the trapped philosopher on an open heath high above the stage merely that we may behold him descending into the fiery pit with solemn pageantry' (13 July 1946). The *Manchester Guardian* critic lamented that some of the devils 'have a touch of Disney about them that is not apt at the moments when Marlowe hoped to chill the blood.'(19 July 1946).

The next Stratford production, however, was a great success, and helped establish the play as a regular part of the Stratford repertory. The company had been reorganized as the RSC in the early 1960s under the direction of Peter Hall, with the goal of producing the work of Shakespeare and his contemporaries alongside the most exciting drama of the present. While most of the contemporary work was done at the company's London Aldwych Theatre, the Stratford productions were invigorated by staging practices and dramaturgical ideas from the 1960s theatre world. Hall's associate directors included John Barton, Peter Brook, and Clifford Williams, who directed *Faustus* at Stratford in 1968. Williams had done Marlowe's *The Jew of Malta* in 1965, a production which established 'that he was not only the RSC's best delineator of the company's house style but also its most resourceful and reliable investigator of forgotten classics' (*Telegraph* 23 August 2005). The same actor, Eric Porter, played the lead in both of Williams's Marlowe productions.

The RSC 'house style' in the 1960s was very influenced by Brecht, with a permanent resident company, spare designs emphasizing the materiality of wood, metal, and leather, and coolly precise verse-speaking that eschewed vocal embellishment. These characteristics came through in a *Faustus* that was complex, ambiguous, and theatrically immediate. Part of the production's power came from the designs of Abd'Elkader Farrah, which combined the medieval iconography of Bosch and Cranach with a Brechtian design aesthetic. The set was a broad circular space that resembled pitted leather, backed by a stark wall. Stark lighting and roughly textured furnishings evoked such different locations as the Pope's chamber and the Emperor's court. Faustus's study featured a suspended human skeleton. A circular screen, framed in metal and depicting Bosch-like images of the Last Judgment, was suspended in front of the set at the beginning and end of the play. Farrah's most distinctive contributions were the Seven Deadly Sins, grotesque cadaverous figures with hideous masks and exaggerated puppet limbs. Gluttony had a huge shaggy belly, walked with crutches, and carried a basket of human skulls on his back. Envy had grasping arms that extended eight feet from his body. Sloth, carried on a litter, had huge feet, and Covetousness's head and hands projected from a metal strongbox. The ugliness of the sins, and Faustus's amused interest in them, gave an index of his distorted moral viewpoint.

The production did not, however, take a simple judgmental approach to Faustus, but nor did it glorify him, as Grotowski's had done. Eric Porter's performance 'did not idealise Faustus or minimize his complexity,' according to William Tydeman, and thus 'perhaps achieved the greatest recent success in conveying the essentially paradoxical nature of the hero's personality' (*Doctor Faustus: Text & Performance*, 53). Irving Wardle complained that his 'patchwork performance … simply takes things as they come … without supplying any connecting thread or suggesting what drove a man of godlike intellect to shut his mind to the prospect of damnation.' (*Times* 27 June 1968). Yet this very lack of consistency led J. C. Trewin to call him 'the most impressive Faustus I have known in the theatre' (*Illustrated London News* 6 July 1968). Trewin felt Porter had 'real authority.' Forty when he played the role, he was able to communicate the pride of youth in the early scenes: 'eagerly and arrogantly resolved, he can suggest the range of the man's questing mind.' In the middle section of the play, Porter went farther than most Faustuses in really enjoying the pranks and conjurations, making them a clue to his character. As William Tydeman described it, 'The keynote of his rendering seemed to be an embittered and weary sense of futility, coupled with a sardonic sense of humour, which worked best in the central scenes where the hero amuses himself cynically at the expense of others' (*Doctor Faustus: Text & Performance*, 61). Porter's relish of these scenes was reinforced by Williams's inventive stagecraft and Farrah's designs. Among the celebrated effects were a hand reaching out of a dish of food at the Pope's banquet, the elegant dance of the silvery phantoms of Alexander and his paramour, and the comic surprise of exploding grape pips spat out by Mephistopheles. These effects kept interest in the performance lively through the challenging middle scenes of the play; B. A. Young felt that 'the height of Clifford Williams's achievement ... is that he has never allowed us to feel this central sagging in the play' (*Financial Times* 28 June 1968).

The most notorious element of the production was the apparition of Helen of Troy, played by Maggie Wright, who appeared completely nude, though covered in gold body paint. In 1968 the Lord Chamberlain's centuries-old powers of censorship were just on the point of relaxing; Helen's entrance marked the first time a naked woman had ever walked across the legitimate stage in Great Britain (more aggressive nudity would follow, in *Hair* and *Oh! Calcutta!* within 2 years). The publicity over the breaking of this taboo nearly overshadowed the production. In the end, the Helen scenes were rather chaste, with Porter kissing Wright rather fastidiously at arm's length, perhaps partly to keep her makeup off his costume.

The end of the production was a celebrated *coup de théâtre*, viscerally terrifying yet in keeping with the slightly detached, existential bent of the production. Nigel Alexander gives a vivid description of Porter's final moments:

> Faustus finished his final speech groveling in abject terror on the ground. The clock finished striking. Nothing happened. After a long moment Faustus raised his head and started to laugh. As he reached the hysteria of relief, the back wall of the stage gave way and fell forward in sections revealing an ominous red glow and a set of spikes like the dragon's teeth of the Siegfried Line. The denizens of hell emerged with a kind of slow continuous shuffle until Faustus was surrounded by a circle of these skeletal figures – including the seven deadly sins. He was then seized and carried shrieking through the teeth of hell mouth which closed leaving the wall of Faustus' study again intact. The actors and the director had thus achieved a notable modern effect which was entirely in keeping with the spirit of the text they were interpreting. (*The Performance of Christopher Marlowe's Dr. Faustus*, 10–11)

The RSC returned to the play only 2 years later in a small-scale version directed by Gareth Morgan for the company's Theatregoround project. While effectively and economically staged, the production lacked power due to David Waller's pedestrian Faustus, 'neither heroic nor sensitive, but obsessively ambitious, coarse, self-indulgent, brainy but unimaginative, a North Country physics professor blunderingly determined to explode the Bomb' (*Guardian*, 31 March 1970). He was easily outshone by the company's rising star Alan Howard, who was 'sad and sinister, insinuating and remote' as Mephistopheles, according to Maureen O'Farrell in the *Dublin Evening Press* (11 March 1970). O'Farrell did find the ending a brilliant *coup de théâtre*: 'Instead of having Faustus hauled off the stage by devils, he merely stands motionless and lets his cloak fall to the ground, a strikingly beautiful symbol in its simplicity of the soul leaving the body.' A similar effect would be used a few years later in the RSC's next major *Faustus*.

RSC (John Barton), 1974

In 1974 John Barton directed an important production for the Royal Shakespeare Company that played at the Edinburgh Festival, as well as in London, Stratford, and on tour. Barton reshaped the play by conflating the two texts, cutting much of the central comic material, and adding over 500 lines derived from *The English Faust Book* and his own imagination. 'I believe that many passages from the Faust-Book can illumine Marlowe's text and accord with it better than can many of the non-Marlovian sections we cut in this production,' he wrote in the program (V&A). Further, Barton set the entire action of the play within Faustus's study, focusing on the beginning and end of Faustus's career, and using a diabolical Chorus to relate his other adventures. He also placed much of the spiritual drama within Faustus's own mind, using puppets to represent the Good and Evil Angels, the Seven Deadly Sins, and a number of other characters.

The setting, by Michael Annals, was a cluttered study with floor-to-ceiling shelving; diagrams in the promptbook show the careful disposition of a large number of properties, including books, horns, baskets, bones, logs, scrolls, casks, jugs, and fire-irons. The curving walls and shadowy recesses also suggested the interior of a skull, promoting the idea of a spiritual monodrama. An hourglass figured prominently on Faustus's desk, and he had a clock with a marching skeleton to mark the hours.

Lucifer spoke the opening chorus, and throughout the play he, Beelzebub, and Mephistopheles recited passages adapted from *The English Faust Book* to comment on Faustus's story. The *Faust Book* material was augmented by Barton to throw attention on a book Faustus was writing:

[Beelzebub]: And this was the beginning of Faustus' book which he ever continued every day of his life for he believed by the setting down of his thoughts and sins, he would in some measure become more able to handle them. In this he erred. In truth, however, the more he searched himself, the more uncertain he became whether he had grown into the thing he was through the temptory of the Devil or through his own tainted nature. (*RSC Promptbook*, 27)

The use of the devilish Chorus allowed Barton to concentrate the action on two moments: Faustus's initial temptation, conjuring, and contract, and his final damnation 24 years later. Before the interval, Ian McKellen's Faustus was a neatly dressed, beardless young man with a mop of brown curls; for the second half of the play he was old, gray, bearded, and weighed down by stained and heavy robes. Most of the comic scenes were cut; there were no Robin and Rafe scenes, no episode with the Pope. At the beginning of the second half, Faustus was just returning from his grand tour (on which he had acquired the Mona Lisa, a prominent prop), and Barton added some rather clumsy lines to account for the Emperor and the Vanholts visiting him in his study:

Since that my fame is spread thro' every land,
That great men come to visit me at home:
Among the rest the Emperor doth come,
Whom I must welcome with some stroke of art.

(*RSC Promptbook*, 28)

The absence of several comic scenes was made up for by an elaboration of the Vanholt business into a tedious sequence of sexual comedy penned by Barton. The pregnant Duchess, charmed by Faustus, made suggestive overtures to him: 'Once by thy art thou didst erect a castle/For my good lord; what will you now erect/To pleasure me?' (*RSC Promptbook*, 54). Their ribald flirtations, briefly interrupted by the Horse-courser and ignored by the oblivious Duke, finally have a payoff when Faustus is accidentally reminded of his doomed state:

Duchess: ... I vow to thee, when spring is come again,
And I am of this tedious burden light,
Then come to me and I shall be thy grove;
And in my garden shall you conjure then,
And we shall be so frolic thou shalt think

Thou art in paradise.
Faustus: Talk not of Paradise.
Duchess: What ails thee, sir?

(*RSC Promptbook*, 55 E–F)

Another effect of having the devils serve as the Chorus was to imply that the deck is heavily stacked against Faustus. 'In their mouths [the Chorus'] traditional exhortations and moralizings sound decidedly wry,' wrote Robert Cushman in the *Observer*. 'It suggests that the whole moral system which Faustus transgresses is diabolically controlled' (1 September 1974). This reading was heightened by having Beelzebub and Mephistopheles play the roles of Valdes and Cornelius, and also by the production's use of puppetry. The Good and Evil Angels seemed to be only phantoms of Faustus's own mind, hand-puppets manipulated by Ian McKellen as he spoke their arguments aloud to himself. Interestingly, at one of the most critical of these junctures, Barton decided to take the burden off McKellen and give it back to the supernatural forces. In the critical passage of 2.3.11–18, in which the Good Angel insists that God will pity Faustus if he repents, but the Evil Angel gloats that Faustus never shall repent, the *Promptbook* originally read 'FAUSTUS takes up the two ANGELS' and had McKellen voice the entire exchange. This approach was crossed out, and a new page added to the text, which makes the exchange one not involving the two angels, but between Faustus and Mephistopheles:

FAUSTUS	If I repent yet, God will pity me.
MEPHISTO.	Thou art a spirit; God cannot pity thee.
FAUSTUS	Yea, God will pity me if I repent.
MEPHISTO.	Ay, but Faustus never shall repent.
FAUSTUS	My heart's so harden'd I cannot repent. (20 A)

Barton evidently decided the scene was not strong enough played as an internal debate, and he called on Emrys James's Mephistopheles to increase the conflict.

James definitely took a back seat to McKellen in this production, mostly watching in a 'cool, ironical and unblinking' manner as Faustus hastened to his end. Having so much of the action played internally may have led to a particularly nervy and mannered performance by McKellen, whose physical and vocal tics were much noted by critics. Billington observed how his 'peculiar acting style, in which his frame seems to be possessed by some emotional Dybbuk, admirably fits the concept of a Faustus who has become a battleground for penitence and despair' (*Guardian*, 6 September 1974); Milton Shulman called it:

> a very busy performance with hardly a moment when the good doctor isn't leaping about for a precious book, nudging the servants of Lucifer for some reaction to his activities, gleefully hugging himself at his own cleverness, or thrashing about in fearful agony as he prepares to meet his doom. A little more repose might make a more convincing philosophical Faustus. (*Evening Standard* 6 September 1974)

Barton used puppets again for the Seven Deadly Sins. William Tydeman described them as 'life-sized marionettes in the Japanese Bunraku tradition, worked by the virtually unseen devils in their black habits' (*Doctor Faustus: Text & Performance*, 76). Their wispy appearance, for Michael Billington, 'underline[d] the illusory nature of Faustus' pleasure' (*Guardian* 6 September 1974). Alexander and his paramour were likewise puppets, as was Helen of Troy, represented by a mask, a blonde wig, and some trailing fabric that McKellen expertly manipulated around the stage. In the case of Helen, Barton was evidently influenced by W. W. Greg's argument that Faustus only seals his damnation through sex with the demon representing her. Barton's text and stage directions emphasize the decisive importance of their coupling:

> (here FAUSTUS takes HELEN to his bed, whereupon MEPHISTOPHELES, after a little while, takes her away again)
> FAUSTUS: Accursed Faustus, what hast thou done?
> Damn'd art thou, Faustus, damn'd; despair and die.
>
> (*RSC Promptbook*, 63)

John Barber objected that using a puppet Helen for this literally climactic moment 'sterilises the ineluctable lure of flesh-and-blood sensuality' (*Telegraph* 9 September 1974), but Jeremy Kingston found it a compelling metaphor: 'Sensuously he fondles that bodyless head's hollow dress: the degradation of the seeker after experience has become complete' (*Punch* 18 September 1974).

Faustus's death also went for psychology rather than spectacle; rather than being dragged to hell by devils, Faustus simply collapsed into despair, becoming himself a lifeless puppet. As David Bevington describes it, 'his twitching body became suddenly lifeless as it sank from his chair, leaving in its wake the empty, shroud-like robe of the once-great scholar' (*Doctor Faustus: A Critical Guide*, 54). In lines adapted from the *Faust Book*, Barton augmented Marlowe's text to deliver a chilling final warning. Beelzebub related that:

> in the house they also found this history written by him, saving only his end, which was after by the scholars thereto added. And thus ended the history of Faustus; out of which example all Christians may learn to fear God and the Devil equally. (*RSC Promptbook*, 73)

The final phrase is pure Barton, and sums up the sense of existential and spiritual doom with which the production was suffused.

RSC (Barry Kyle), 1989

Barry Kyle's 1989 production of *Doctor Faustus* for the Royal Shakespeare Company was his second production of Marlowe in the new Swan Theatre in Stratford, which opened in 1986 under Kyle's artistic directorship. He had directed *The Jew of Malta* in 1987 in a richly comic and satirical production featuring eclectic costuming, creative use of the Swan's three-tiered structure, and a dominant performance by Alun Armstrong as Barabas. Kyle's *Faustus* was a much more austere and focused production, which unified the play with severe monochromatic designs, an all-male cast, a choric approach to character, and a tight 2-hour running time, playing the A-text straight through without an interval.

The design, by Ashley Martin-Davis, was rather at odds with the atmosphere of the new Swan, with its warm galleries of honey-colored wood. The Swan's stage and *frons scenae* were encased in grim, unbroken surfaces of ashy gray. The production was actually more at home when it transferred to The Pit in London, an aptly named concrete bunker in the bowels of the Barbican Centre that the RSC used for small-scale transfers. The Swan did allow Kyle to exploit the vertical dimensions of the play's design, with Faustus attempting to ascend a ladder to a heavenly doorway, only to be lowered, in a cruciform cage, to the pit of hell below the stage's trap doors.

The production began with a demonic Chorus emerging from the trap, reciting the lines of the prologue individually and then in unison. Ten young, athletic male actors played all of the play's roles except for Faustus, Mephistopheles, and Wagner. They began the play as devils writhing up from the pit, became Faustus's fellow scholars during his opening speech, and enacted all of the supporting characters with only a few suggestive costume pieces. Shirtless, in red pyjama trousers, sometimes donning robes of scarlet, gray, or black, they were evidently a demonic force throughout the play, which seemed to be set entirely in hell, or in Faustus's mind. The chorus's continual presence gave cohesion to the production, and here and there added a whiff of homoeroticism, with a sexually aggressive devil-bride and a broad-shouldered male Helen of Troy. They also helped integrate the central comic interludes, which passed efficiently, though without much mirth, to the strains of Ilona Sekacz's Kurt Weill-like music.

The Chorus's most striking moment was a representation of the Seven Deadly Sins. Seven of the actors formed a single scrum-like entity, with one emerging from the corporate body to characterize each individual sin. Pride struggled and clambered out of the mass in his hunger for predominance; Envy stood apart sulkily from a group embrace, drawing an audience laugh as he announced his name. Gluttony was a devouring, defecating monster through which the individual devils passed, recalling the birth scene in Richard Schechner's *Dionysus in '69*. One devil, left on the floor in Gluttony's wake, was kicked and discovered to be the sleeping Sloth. Such elements of the production excited some critics, but others felt they belonged too much to the theatrical experiments of an earlier generation. Michael Coveney complained that the production 'smack[ed] of drama class exercises and ghastly fringe grope-ins of two decades ago' (*Financial Times* 12 May 1989).

The youngish Faustus was Gerard Murphy, a sturdily built, blond-haired actor whose physical presence suggested contemporary earthiness and vigor rather than Renaissance intellectual yearning. Some critics found him wanting in sophistication, but Michael Billington praised him for 'remind[ing] us that Faustus is, exactly like Marlowe, a working-class scholarship boy' and 'imply[ing] spirituality under a bullish exterior' (*Country Life* 18 May 1989). Dressed in white robes, Murphy gave a physically and emotionally committed performance, remaining on stage throughout the play in a state of unrelieved tension. He gained no pleasure from his supernatural powers. He performed his conjuring tricks with gloomy anguish, and even before he had finished his paean to the muscular Helen, she was already leaving the stage, her robe slipping from his grasp as he fell to the floor. His final monologue was played slowly and quietly, with painful intensity but little poetic range or richness.

Spiritual dimensions were more fully realized by David Bradley's mesmerizing Mephistopheles, whose age, gravity, and stillness set him apart from the energetic ensemble. A gaunt, hawk-faced actor described by multiple critics as 'cadaverous' and 'saturnine,' he managed to express the torments of hell in his dry and steely voice. When he first appeared to Faustus, it was not as a dragon or demon, but as a thorn-crowned and suffering Christ-figure. 'He has clearly seen and felt terrors that no one else has,' John Peter reported (*Sunday Times* 14 May 1989). Charles Spencer wrote, 'He has the blank face of a washed-up comedian, alone in his dressing room after a particularly bad night, and his voice is drained of expression except when he speaks of the misery of hell' (*Telegraph* 28 November 1989). Irving Wardle captured some of the key moments in Bradley's performance:

> As he says, he is in hell; and not for a second, even when consulting a map and acting as bored tourist guide in Rome, does he ever let you forget it. Whether debating cosmology or stealing the Pope's dinner, he is consumed by inner torment. Not for nothing is he dressed as a mendicant friar; he is a beggar, thirsting for Faustus' soul, and when he obtains it he kisses his victim's hand in pure gratitude, and smiles his only smile as the pain, for an instant, remits. Unforgettable. (*Times* 12 May 1989)

The other notable performance came from Richard McCabe as Wagner, the only other character set apart from the Chorus of demons. Though a skilled comic actor, McCabe played the part not for laughs but as a sneering malcontent, rather like the Flamineo (from Webster's *The White Devil*) he played for the RSC in 1995–6. He menaced the scholars with his puritanical preachings, terrorized the hapless Clown, and mockingly echoed Faustus's praises of the sights from his grand tour. He sardonically narrated the choral passages about Faustus's mid-play adventures, then lolled insolently in Faustus's chair, wearing a pointed dunce cap, to observe the antics of Robin and Rafe. His constant, baleful presence made him seem a part of the sinister conspiracy against Faustus, and indeed he was given the play's last word. After Faustus's descent to hell, Mephistopheles spoke the first four lines of the final chorus, with the whole company intoning the words, 'Faustus is gone.' Then Wagner, who had been leaning on Faustus's chair, violently overturned it, savagely shouting out the Latin tag that concludes the A-text (and which was presumably never meant for performance): *'Terminat hora diem, terminat author opus.'* This innovation, suggesting that perhaps Wagner is the devilish author who is here concluding his work, ironically foreshadowed an event in the actor's career. In the next major British production of *Doctor Faustus*, at the Old Vic in 2002, Richard McCabe played not Wagner, but Mephistopheles.

Young Vic, 2002

The chief selling point of the Young Vic's *Doctor Faustus* was the appearance of Jude Law in the title role. The 29-year-old film star played Faustus for director David Lan, with whom he had previously done Ford's *'Tis Pity She's a Whore*. Law's glamorous presence guaranteed a sell-out as well as some critical backlash; it was McCabe's chilly Mephistopheles that garnered most of the praise.

The production owed much to Grotowski, using a small ensemble, a stripped-down setting, and a mixture of period and modern clothes. The set was a high, narrow catwalk cutting diagonally across the octagonal arena of the Young Vic, with the audience sitting on either side. A blue vault with suspended planets suggested the heavens above, while hell was a slag-strewn ditch into which characters tossed props as the play proceeded. Law's Faustus began the play in scholar's robe and black doublet, but discarded these as the play went on, finishing in a loose white shirt and modern jeans. In his opening monologue, he contemptuously flung Aristotle and Galen into the pit. Law was an angry, bitter Faustus, arrogant and bored, not particularly animated by a desire for new knowledge but fed up with things as they were. Critics characterized him variously as a 'hedonistic playboy,' 'a joylessly pleasure-seeking "rakehell",' and 'a spoilt brat and rebel,' perhaps responding somewhat to Law's public image as well as his onstage demeanor (Kate Stratton, *Time Out*, 27 March 2002; Paul

Taylor, *Independent*, 20 March 2002; Kate Bassett, *Independent on Sunday*, 24 March 2002). The production played to the sense of Faustus as a young narcissist. He took the role of Pride during the Seven Deadly Sins episode, and rather than conjuring a visible Helen of Troy, Law apostrophized, and then kissed his own image in a mirror.

Both moments may have derived in part from the economies of the production, which used only five actors in addition to the two leads. The relentless doubling and low-tech staging resulted in some rather clunky effects; methods that were revolutionary in Grotowski's day struck millennial critics as hackneyed and tiresome. Charles Spencer lamented 'some horrid outbreaks of clichéd physical theatre' (*Mail on Sunday* 31 March 2002), and Georgina Brown decried the 'cringe-making mask-acting and physical performances unworthy of a drama workshop' (*Telegraph* 19 March 2002). The Seven Deadly Sins, like those in Kyle's production, were played as a single metamorphosing entity, but without much originality or flair.

The best scenes were those focused on the two leads, which played effectively on the catwalk stage. The famously handsome Law was a charismatic, kinetic young Faustus. As Mephistopheles, Richard McCabe exploited the smirking menace he had used as Wagner in Kyle's production. Spencer described him as having 'the face of a debauched cherub' (*Mail on Sunday* 31 March 2002), and his gloating, icily still presence complemented Law's frenetic energy. McCabe had occasional bursts of startling intensity. When Mephistopheles and Faustus were disputing about astronomy, each rapidly scribbled mathematical calculations on chalkboard walls at the ends of the catwalk. McCabe's 'this is hell' speech was an angry rant, and at the end he shouted about having entrapped Faustus with vindictive glee.

Faustus's final moments were played enigmatically, suggesting that his damnation was a state of mind rather than a medieval torment. After an intensely committed monologue of sweat and tears, Faustus looked up perplexed to see the scholars enter and begin intoning the final chorus. He initially laughed with relief, then froze as they declared, 'Faustus is gone.' Mephistopheles entered slowly and offered a book to Faustus, which he accepted with his final words, 'Ah, Mephistopheles.' He held the book to his head, then slumped to the stage, contemplating the book in solitude as the lights fell. The production implied that hell was an existential isolation, a Beckettian half-life of which this Faustus was only beginning to become aware.

Chichester Festival Theatre, 2004

In 2004 the Minerva Theatre in Chichester staged an unusual peripatetic performance that culminated in the city's great cathedral. Designed as a community outreach project, the production incorporated over 100 townspeople and students. Recalling Faustus's medieval antecedents, the mystery play cycles, the Chichester *Faustus* promenaded through the streets of the city, involving the audience in a spiritual drama that engaged with the quotidian as well as the eternal. The performance began in the theatre, with Samuel West's Faustus, a bored modern student in jeans and trainers, smoking pot and sniffing glue while dismissing the various branches of traditional learning. An actor known for his elegant diction, West made the bold choice of playing a Faustus marked by his speech as 'base of stock.' As Kate Bassett commented, 'Perhaps mindful of Marlowe's own roots – the son of a shoemaker turned Cambridge scholar – West speaks his ravishing poetry with a rough estuary accent' (*Independent on Sunday* 19 September 2004). Mephistopheles, played by Michael Feast, was a contemporary clergyman who took a syringe out of his briefcase to extract Faustus's blood for the pact.

After Faustus signed the deed, performers and audience moved out into the Chichester shopping district, where the Seven Deadly Sins disported themselves in appropriate locations, with Covetousness, for instance, crying out for his gold while embracing an automatic teller machine. Angels hung from hotel balconies, Lucifer appeared in a red MG convertible, and student devils snarled from shop doorways as the audience made their way toward the cathedral. The results were mixed, according to John Peter: 'The promenade becomes quite jolly, you smile at each other in polite embarrassment, as one does, and the play's tension, anger and black humour disappears' (*Sunday Times* 19 September 2014). In keeping with the rhythm of the play, however, the final scenes in the cathedral were much more serious. Helen of Troy appeared in gold on the flying buttresses outside; the angels called down from the echoey heights of the cathedral. Faustus's final speech, delivered by West with harrowing intensity in the stone-vaulted nave, was punctuated by the tolling of the cathedral bell. *The Times* hailed the production as 'a civic achievement that brings one close, at least in imagination, to what city theatre may have been like 500 years ago' (13 September 2004).

Shakespeare's Globe Theatre (Dominic Dromgoole), 2011

In 2011 Shakespeare's Globe Theatre staged *Doctor Faustus* in their conjecturally reconstructed playhouse on the South Bank of the Thames. While scholars had raised questions about the dimensions of the Globe and the way it was used, the first performance of *Doctor Faustus* in the space nonetheless marked an important moment in the theatrical history of the play. Globe Artistic Director Dominic Dromgoole included *Faustus* in a conceptual season entitled 'The Word is God' and commencing with a reading of the full text of the King James Bible in commemoration of its 400th anniversary. The season also included a staging of Tony Harrison's version of a medieval mystery cycle, so *Faustus* was performed in the context of both medieval theatricality and Reformation Christianity.

The production was marked, above all, by inventive and spectacular staging, employing puppetry developed by Steve Tiplady of the Little Angel Theatre. Where Marlowe only mentions flying dragons, Dromgoole had Faustus and Mephistopheles mounted on huge skeletal puppets resembling fossilized pterosaurs, with flapping wings operated by the Chorus of black-clad scholar/devils. Masked and goat-horned stilt walkers turned Robin and Dick into a dog and ape with realistic animal heads. The Good Angel wore Joan-of-Arc armor and huge white wings, and repeatedly fought her red-clad enemy with a samurai sword. For all these effects, the production had difficulty building a sense of cosmic conflict. As Brian Logan observed in the *Guardian*, 'You leave feeling you have plumbed the contents of the theatre's wardrobe department, not the depths of the spiritual abyss' (24 June 2011). More than one critic commented on the difficulty of creating an atmosphere of supernatural terror on an open stage in broad daylight – a challenge Henslowe's company presumably had to overcome as well.

Director Dromgoole used his own conflation of the A- and B-texts, maximizing comedy as well as spectacle. The *Time Out* review noted that 'As so often at the Globe, the comedy carries better than the tragedy' (27 June 2011). The text was sometimes rewritten to provide comic opportunities, especially for Robin. A running joke was made out of his malapropisms in the encounter with Wagner; so he not only said 'gridirons' for 'guilders' but also 'goujons' and 'gridders.' Balliol and Belcher became 'Boneyole and Belfry' and 'Bananaho and Bucket.' Both devils were puppets, one of which erupted from the seat of Robin's pants. Pierce Quigley won high praise for his performance of Robin, though Charles Spencer, of the *Telegraph*, was severe: 'If you think Shakespeare's clowns are unfunny, just try enduring Marlowe's for a couple of hours' (27 June 2011).

Quigley was a crowd favorite for his ad libbing and interacting with the audience – not out of keeping with the spirit of the play's comic scenes, and part of the culture at the Globe. Among Dromgoole's other innovations were combining the Vintner with the Hostess (allowing some coarse sexual comedy during her search for the goblet) and bringing Nan Spit onstage to flirt with Dick. More raunchy humor, again perhaps in the spirit of the play, was provided by the devil-bride, who had grotesque pendulous breasts and a sparkling firework at her crotch. And when Faustus fetched grapes for the Duchess, he did it without Mephistopheles's help, instead reaching under her skirts and pulling them out from between her legs, to her evident delight.

The central performances were found by many to be a little lukewarm; Henry Hitchings felt there was 'too little frisson between the leads' (*Standard* 24 June 2011). Paul Hilton was a young, vain Faustus, 'too laid back' in the view of Kate Bassett (*Independent on Sunday* 26 September 2011). Michael Coveney, one of the strongest advocates of the production, admitted Hilton was 'not as lyrically magnificent as you'd like,' but felt he had a 'hard-bitten, restless heroic quality that keeps you hooked' (*Independent* 28 June 2011). He was visually linked to Arthur Darvill's Mephistoheles: both were young, lean, bearded, and dressed in Renaissance doublets for most of the action (the lines about Mephistopheles being dressed as an 'old Franciscan friar' were cut). Darvill was known to audiences as the sidekick to TV's Doctor Who, played in that incarnation by Matt Smith. This celebrity was presumably one of the reasons for his casting, and he played the role in a similar way, as a time-traveling boon-companion who seemed to reliably partner Faustus through his adventures. Dromgoole put special emphasis on the moment of Mephistopheles's final turning on Faustus, in one of the production's most dramatic directorial choices. Rather than having

Faustus dragged to hell at the end of his last soliloquy, Dromgoole significantly rearranged the final sequence in a way not warranted by either existing text.

Hilton's Faustus was not visibly aged by his 24 years of adventures, though he walked with a cane and was more richly dressed, wearing a heavy robe based on the robes of Henry VIII. He seemed drunk in his conversation with the scholars about Helen of Troy. She appeared initially as an oversized diaphanous puppet, out of which Sarita Piotrowski emerged to embrace Faustus. Hilton's delivery of the famous apostrophe was entirely without lyricism; he retained some of his drunkenness and shouted about Menelaus, Achilles, and 'flaming Jupiter' with mocking aggression. As he left the stage with Helen, the Good Angel came forward and made her speech from B. 5.2 about leaving Faustus. Lucifer and Beelzebub entered but did not speak, and Faustus returned with the scholars, stripping off his rich garments as he bemoaned the 'vain pleasure' of his life. Dressed only in breeches and white shirt, he began his final soliloquy. Near the end of this, just before the final striking of the clock, Mephistopheles entered for a lengthy exchange with Faustus, incorporating not only his gloating remarks about having led Faustus away from salvation, but the Bad Angel's speech about the torments of hell. Only after this fairly substantial scene did Faustus speak his final six lines about being turned to water drops and burning his books. The devils entered, carrying what appeared to be bloody skeletal babies, and carried Faustus back through the discovery space. There was no scholar scene, nor any severed limbs; Wagner spoke the final chorus, and the performance ended with an exuberant jig, in the Globe tradition.

Twenty-first century adaptations

Four and a quarter centuries after its first performance, Marlowe's *Doctor Faustus* continues to be performed throughout the world. Sometimes the Faustus story is the inspiration for an entirely new play, as in the case of Goethe's *Faust*, Gertrude Stein's elliptical modernist libretto *Doctor Faustus Lights the Lights* (which ends with Marlowe's Helen speech), or Vaclav Havel's 1986 Czech political parable *Temptation*. Several recent plays have drawn inspiration from Marlowe or blended his text with new material. In 2004, play-wright Ben Power interspersed Faustus's story with that of the icon-oclastic Young British Artists, the Chapman brothers, who as an artistic statement bought and defaced a set of Goya's etchings *The Disasters of War*. Directed by Rupert Goold for Headlong Theatre, Power's *Faustus* used the parallel stories to raise questions about creative freedom, ethics, and authenticity. The same year, American playwright David Mamet, in his play *Faustus*, reworked Marlowe to explore the personal hell of a self-centered academic whose intel-lectual pride costs him his family (the play was originally written for Jude Law, who chose to do Marlowe's version instead). David Davalos's 2008 comedy *Wittenberg* depicts Faustus as a freethinking professor and rival of Martin Luther; the two carry out a kind of *psychomachia* over the young Danish prince Hamlet. A 2013 joint production by the West Yorkshire Playhouse and the Glasgow Citizens' Theatre featured two new acts by Colin Teevon, to replace Faustus's mid-play grand tour. In Dominic Hill's production, Kevin Trainor's Faustus became a Vegas-style celebrity magician led to destruction by Siobhan Redmond's Mephistopheles, his diabolical female assistant.

Productions using Marlowe's text may be adapted to other historical or political circumstances. At the University of North Carolina in 2007, Andrew James Hartley directed the play as the story of a bored middle-aged academic who aspires to be a rock star. A 2013 production in El Paso, Texas set the play in the time of the Mexican Emperor Maximilian, connecting the bargain with the Devil to traditional practices associated with the Day of the Dead. For the 450th anniversary of Marlowe's birth in 2014, a number of prominent theatres performed *Doctor Faustus*, including the Marlowe Theatre in his native Canterbury, the Marlowe Society at Cambridge University, the Rose theatre on Bankside (where the first recorded performance occurred), and the American Shakespeare Center in Virginia. It seems certain that Marlowe's play will continue to inspire theatre-makers with its fable of temptation, magic, and damnation.

5   The Play on Screen

Like Marlowe's other plays, *Doctor Faustus* has had relatively little life on the screen. While there are many treatments of the Faust legend on film, Marlowe's play has not attracted filmmakers. The only major cinematic version of *Doctor Faustus* is that starring Richard Burton and Elizabeth Taylor (1967), based on the Oxford stage production by Nevill Coghill. The innovative Czech filmmaker Jan Švankmajer made a 1994 film *Faust* that incorporates Marlowe's play into a visually arresting modern version of the legend, featuring puppetry and stop-motion animation. The 2011 production from Shakespeare's Globe has been released on video in a version filmed before a live audience. With the increasing interest in Marlowe's work along with the proliferation of alternative, more widely accessible methods of videography, it may be hoped that screen versions of *Doctor Faustus* may become more numerous and varied. In the meantime, the existing versions all have interest for students of the play.

The Burton/Taylor film (1967)

When Burton and Taylor were working with Nevill Coghill on the 1966 production at the Oxford Playhouse, they conceived the idea of turning it into a film, which came to fruition the following year. Filming was done at Dino de Laurentis's studios in Rome, with Burton and Coghill co-directing; it was Burton's first directorial effort. Along with Burton and Taylor, members of the Oxford University Dramatic Society rounded out the youthful supporting cast, with Andreas Teuber repeating his role as Mephistopheles.

The film was universally panned on its release, with Renata Adler, in the *NY Times*, declaring that it 'is of an awfulness that bends the mind' (7 February 1968). While some of the criticism is justified, the film contains much of value, especially its record of Burton's burned-out, steely-voiced performance of the leading role. Many of the cinematic choices, though unsuccessful, are interesting, particularly the decision to import material from Marlowe's other plays into the film, which had not been done in the stage production.

Shot entirely on soundstages, the Burton/Taylor *Faustus* has a somewhat garish, horror-film look, with gloomy spider-webbed sets and lurid-colored lighting. The film introduces Faustus as an aging scholar, with long, thinning gray hair and absurd round spectacles. He is receiving academic honors and being cheered by his students, but he is clearly dissatisfied with his life. Alone in his chamber, he rejects the traditional forms of learning in an opening soliloquy delivered partly in voice-over. Furtively, he fetches a chest of magical appurtenances from a hidden space under the floorboards to begin his conjurations. As in the stage production, Burton plays the Faustus of the opening scenes as an unromantic figure, a fussy and repressed little man in an unflattering short jerkin. The Good and Evil Angels are only heard as voices, the former seeming to emanate from a carved St Sebastian, the latter from a skull on Faustus's desk. As the Evil Angel entices Faustus, he looks into the eye of the skull and sees a bevy of nude women, eliciting a leering laugh from him. When a young and glamorous Valdes and Cornelius tempt him with the notion of 'women, or unwedded maids,' he looks in a crystal and has his first vision of Elizabeth Taylor. Taylor was a major Hollywood star, widely considered one of the world's most beautiful women. She plays various versions of feminine temptation for Faustus: not only Helen, but the devil-bride, Alexander's paramour, and finally the laughing demon who pulls him into hell. Clearly, Burton's Faustus is not driven by intellectual hubris but by sensual desire. Like Burton himself, he is unable to resist the destructive pull of earthly pleasures.

Mephistopheles, by contrast, is a reserved and ascetic figure. Andreas Teuber was an Oxford undergraduate when he first took on the role (he went on to a Harvard Ph.D. and an academic career in philosophy). With a shaven head, grave demeanor, and youthful voice, he seems like an earnest seminarian rather than an 'old Franciscan friar.' As Mephistopheles reads out the terms of the contract, Faustus is seen to grow younger through cinematic effect, becoming a vigorous man with ruddy complexion and short brown hair.

The film's central sequence is an elaboration of the pageant of the Seven Deadly Sins that incorporates other Marlovian (and non-Marlovian) texts. After hearing from Lucifer that 'In hell is all manner of delight,' Faustus finds himself in a cheesy verdant soundstage bower, being guided by a lipsticked male Lechery through a 'garden of delights.' Faustus encounters Covetousness in a golden cage, and learns that he is bound up by 'infinite riches in a little room' (from *The Jew of Malta*). He declares 'I must have wanton poets, pleasant wits,' and launches into Gaveston's hedonistic speech from *Edward II*, which is augmented with slow-motion homoerotic gymnastics. When he mentions 'Actaeon, peeping through a grove,' Taylor appears again as Diana. Faustus engages Wrath in a broadsword combat, behind which is superimposed the cavalry charge from Olivier's film of *Henry V*. Triumphantly, Faustus declares in the words of Tamburlaine, 'Is it not passing brave to be a king,/And ride in triumph through Persepolis?' While this is a sequence to which Renata Adler's severe criticism might apply, it takes a strong position on Faustus's fleshly weaknesses.

The low-life scenes with Robin, the Horse-courser, and so forth are entirely cut, but the film does make some grim attempts at comedy. Accompanied by Mephistopheles in feline form, Faustus conjures for the Emperor and his wife (who speaks some of the lines of the Duchess of Vanholt) and bests the haughty Knight, whose horns shrink back into his head with another special effect. As Alexander's paramour, Taylor is completely covered in silver makeup, with a mop-like wig of metallic curls (Adler describes her as 'frosted all over ... like a pastry, or a devaluated refugee from "Goldfinger".') The mockery of the Pope is accomplished with not one but two custard-pie gags, as well as a chorus of simpering friars in pancake makeup and white tonsures. It is the sort of sequence that might work on stage in front of a live audience but seems grotesquely forced on film. Burton's Faustus, perhaps purposefully, is repellently nasty in the scene, making fart noises with the vicious glee of a misbehaving schoolboy. The sequence has a payoff in a chilling final moment, when the friars' white cloaks suddenly stand empty and threatening, then collapse as Faustus flails at them in a savage frenzy.

Faustus's degeneration is expressed through a drunken tavern scene in which he leads a chorus of the drinking song from *Gammer Gurton's Needle* and then beats the landlord, crying, 'I'll show you tricks, you lying sot, knave, cuckold!' Staggering to his feet after passing out, he leans on an hourglass (repeatedly used in the film as a reminder of Faustus's numbered days), and mutters, 'What art thou, Faustus, but a man condemned to die?' After bequeathing his goods to a boyish Wagner and dismissing a youngish Old Man, Faustus conjures Helen for the Scholars. After all of the foreshadowing and sneak previews of Taylor's Helen, her climactic scene makes relatively little impression. In a tight two-shot embrace, Burton intones his panegyric while Taylor stares glassily upward past him. The implication of the film is that she is the agent of his destruction throughout (echoing both W. W. Greg's succubus theory and a popular narrative of Taylor's impact on Burton's career as a classical actor). When Faustus rises from bed with Helen, he can no longer see himself in a mirror: he has become a spirit doomed to imminent damnation.

Burton delivers Faustus's final speech in a highly theatrical manner, presumably much as he did it on the Oxford stage, with a fully projected stage voice and frantic gestures. Against a green-screened backdrop of stars, he shouts 'I'll leap up to my God!' The cinematic effect of Christ's blood streaming in the firmament is actually pretty effective, an instance of the way film can convey an image for which the Elizabethan theatre depended on words and imagination. The floor of Faustus's study opens to reveal a vaguely Boschian hell, with animal-headed devils whipping half-naked sinners. Taylor appears again as an agent of Faustus's destruction, this time a cackling, snake-crowned demon with green skin and bright red lips, who embraces Faustus and pulls him down into hell. The young Mephistopheles watches, his face impassive but his cheeks streaked with tears. In a sophisticated interpretation of the film, Pascale Aebischer asserts that:

> Andreas Teuber's terse and restrained performance as Mephistopheles can … be read as an intradiegetic condemnation of the film's excesses, as he despairingly shakes his head at the foolishness of Faustus's wavering and his easy subjection to the sexual allure of a woman who has obliterated his intellectual ambitions. ('Renaissance Tragedy on Film', 118)

The film ends with a page from an illuminated Bible declaring 'Stipendium peccati mors est,' and Burton's voice-over intoning 'The reward of sin is death': a severe final judgment in a film that never goes easy on Faustus, nor on the Burton/Taylor myth.

Švankmajer's *Faust* (1994)

Jan Švankmajer's 1994 Czech film *Faust* is a fairly free adaptation, but Marlowe's play provides its basic outline and much of its text. The film also includes aspects of Goethe's play, Gounod's opera, and Christian Dietrich Grabbe's 1828 *Don Juan and Faust*, as well as Czech puppet theatre. Švankmajer is a renowned animator with a striking, rather sinister visual imagination, and his style is appropriate to the supernatural world of the play. Most of the film is live action, but it contains sequences of animation and puppetry.

The film is set in contemporary Prague, and begins with a long, wordless prologue in which a drab, middle-aged businessman-type, played by Petr Čepek, is handed a map directing him to a derelict building, which turns out to be a theatre. In a dressing room he finds and puts on the costume and makeup of Faustus, and reads out a short, doggerel version of his opening soliloquy to himself in a mirror. The Good and Evil Angels are life-size marionettes in a puppet theatre representing Faustus's study. Valdes and Cornelius, who gave Faustus the map, are virtually the only other human characters. After a lengthy conjuring sequence, Faustus successfully raises Mephistopheles, initially a claymation demon who has Faustus's face. They exchange much of the dialogue from Marlowe's 1.3 and 2.3. There are lengthy sequences of stop-motion animation and puppetry, as well as surreal sequences on the streets of Prague. Apart from Faustus, characters are mainly represented by puppets or by live actors with puppet heads.

Švankmajer intended the film as a political parable of Czech history and its various pacts with the Devil: 'Faust has passively accepted capitalism as easily as he used to swallow totalitarianism' (*NY Times*, 26 October 1994). Faustus eventually finds himself conjuring a pageant of David and Goliath for the King of Portugal. Helen is created when a new head is placed on the marionette devil's body; we see the Devil's feet while Faustus is having sex with her. In the end, Faustus tries to flee the theatre as the last hour is ticking by on his wristwatch, but he is struck and killed by a car on the street. As he is leaving, we see another man entering with the same map; presumably he will be the next victim. As the dead Faustus lies under the car, an Old Man pulls off one of his legs, in a macabre version of the Horse-courser's trick, and scuttles away with it wrapped in newspaper. The whole film has a feel of Kafkaesque menace and absurdity, and Faustus is a hapless victim rather than a defiant rebel or tragic figure. Švankmajer's *Faust* is strange but compelling, and provides a fascinating interpretation of Marlowe's *Doctor Faustus* in an ironic modernist mode.

Shakespeare's Globe (2011)

The Globe production discussed in Chapter 4 is now available on DVD and online through Globe Player (https://globeplayer.tv/videos/doctor-faustus). This is an elaborately produced video recording of a live performance, with multiple camera angles, careful editing of both image and sound, and a mixture of close-ups and wide shots, including audience reactions. It gives one an impression of seeing the play at the Globe, but controls the viewer's point of view much more than would be the case at an actual production. The costumes are eclectic but suggestive of the play's period, and the architecture of the Globe is frequently visible. This video version is valuable in communicating something of the effect of the play as performed in an early modern playhouse, but it is very much a twenty-first century artifact. Close-ups occasionally reveal tiny microphones attached to the actors' heads, and some of the puppetry and movement work, especially by the chorus of Scholars, comes across as self-consciously contemporary.

The generally broad and energetic playing style generates plenty of laughter from the audience. The faces of the groundlings, who appear to be mainly college students, are often visible; they smile up at the actors, or cringe away shrieking from such gags as Robin's feigned urination or the Horse-courser's stripping off his wet clothes. Even a moment as ostensibly serious as the torture of the antipope Bruno gets an audience laugh when his tormentors pretend to pull out his tongue and fling it in the crowd. (The text is a conflation, favoring the B-text.)

The fact that the actors are playing to 1500 people in a large outdoor space means that their voices are sometimes rather forced and flattened out by filmic standards. This is somewhat to the disadvantage of Paul Hilton's Faustus, who speaks a high percentage of the play's text, and comes across as rather strained and lacking in nuance. Arthur Darvill's Mephistopheles, by contrast, makes a strong impression through his often silent presence. The video frequently cuts to him for close-up reaction shots; his weary, pensive demeanor manages to convey both cool menace and a level of sympathy, even intimacy, with Faustus.

Several moments come across very effectively in the video version. Pearce Quigley's Robin has a restrained, deadpan quality that plays as well on video as in the theatre. The Seven Deadly Sins are both funny and disturbing, emerging from traps below the stage under the whip of an imposing horned Beelzebub. The gag of Benvolio's cutting off Faustus's head is convincing, though it is a purely theatrical effect. The final sequence, which highlights Mephistopheles's betrayal of Faustus (moved to near the end of Faustus's soliloquy), has considerable impact. After Faustus is carried back through the discovery space, however, the performance concludes with some rather gratuitous touches that probably will not age well. The enfeebled Lucifer regains his strength as the company carries out giant puppet wings to attach to his back. Then, after the curtain call, the company does a labored jig involving puppet devil-babies, gold megaphones, and a lute duel between Faustus and Mephistopheles. There are similar moments throughout the performance, which make the video-viewer very conscious of not being part of the theatrical audience. Nonetheless, the Globe video version provides a useful record of the play being staged under quasi-Elizabethan conditions, while also demonstrating its vitality as a piece of twenty-first century performance.

6 Critical Assessments

Important topics in *Faustus* criticism have included the uncertainties around the two texts; the theological questions surrounding Faustus's failure to repent; the relationship between Marlowe's allegedly transgressive beliefs and the play's value system; and the play's inheritances from medieval dramaturgy. In a way, these issues all relate to the central question of how we assess Faustus: as a justly damned sinner or a heroic Renaissance Humanist. Judgments of Faustus, in turn, are often rooted in judgments of Marlowe.

Early criticism

There are only a few mentions of Marlowe by other writers during his own short lifetime, and most reflect negatively on Marlowe's alleged beliefs while acknowledging his gifts as a writer. Two are by Robert Greene, a disgruntled, failed playwright who is best known for denigrating Shakespeare as an 'upstart crow' with a 'tiger's heart wrapped in a player's hide.' He also had a quarrel with Marlowe, and in a preface to his 1588 work *Perimedes the Blacksmith*, he complained that his own work had been disparaged 'for that I could not make my verses jet upon the stage in tragical buskins … daring God out of heaven with that atheist *Tamburlaine*.' Marlowe, who had achieved great popularity with *Tamburlaine*'s debut on the English stage a few months before, was evidently already associated with atheism and other sinful vices. Greene goes on to revile 'such mad and scoffing poets, that have prophetical spirits as bold as Merlin's race.' 'Merlin' is not only an allusion to the Arthurian magician but a common version of Marlowe's name; and his 'mad and scoffing' spirit is attributed by Greene to 'self-love' or 'too much frequenting the hot-house,' suggesting venereal disease. In his *Groatsworth of Wit* (1592), along with his attack on Shakespeare, Greene again castigates Marlowe for atheism, as well as 'pestilent Machiavellian policy.' Henry Chettle, another Elizabethan playwright, though he confessed to 'reverence' for Marlowe's learning, did not wish to know him personally on account of his alleged atheism. Finally, Thomas Kyd, author of *The Spanish Tragedy*, gave evidence to the Privy Council about 'Marlowe's monstrous opinions' after heretical writings were found in Kyd's room. He alleged that they belonged to Marlowe, who was killed around the same time. Evidently his reputation for atheism made his fellow playwrights want to distance themselves from Marlowe.

Marlowe's death prompted differing reactions from his colleagues. Francis Meres, one of the first English literary critics, moralized that 'our tragical poet Marlowe for his Epicurism and atheism had a tragical death'; yet he gave Marlowe his due, along with Shakespeare, as among 'our best for tragedy' (*Palladis Tamia*, 1598). Some Elizabethan writers remembered him fondly as 'kind Kit Marlowe' (John Marston), 'the Muses' darling' (George Peele), or 'poor deceased Kit Marlowe' (Thomas Nashe). Others praised him as a 'pure, elemental wit' who was 'renowned for his rare art' (Thomas Thorpe, Thomas Heywood). Ben Jonson, though he thought Marlowe fell short of Shakespeare, nonetheless gave an indelible characterization of his verse style in referring to 'Marlowe's mighty line.' Shakespeare seems to recall Marlowe warmly in *As You Like It* when Phoebe, quoting *Hero and Leander*, says 'Dead shepherd, now I find thy saw of might,/Whoever loved, that loved not at first sight.' (*Norton Shakespeare*, 1997, 3.5.81–2). Michael Drayton gave the most eloquent encomium:

> … Marlowe, bathed in Thespian springs
> Had in him those brave translunary things,
> That the first poets had, his raptures were
> All air, and fire, which made his verses clear
> For that fine madness still he did retain,
> Which rightly should possess a poet's brain.
>
> (*Elegy to Henry Reynolds*, 105–10)

None of these remembrances address *Doctor Faustus* specifically, but the mixture of admiration for Marlowe's poetic gifts and concern for his dangerous opinions would have been a likely response to the play as well as its author. Though the story of Faustus can be taken as an orthodox moral exemplum, the theatrical legends surrounding its early performances, discussed in Chapter 1, suggest that his contemporaries thought Marlowe was once again playing with fire. Interestingly, the one direct allusion to *Doctor Faustus* by Shakespeare invokes the play's comic elements. In *The Merry Wives of Windsor*, Bardolph complains of how some ostensibly German cozeners stole the host's horses: 'they threw me off from behind one of them, in a slough of mire; and set spurs and away, like three German devils, three Doctor Faustuses.' (*Norton Shakespeare*, 1997, 4.5.54–6). The incident recalls both the Horse-courser and the fate of Benvolio and his companions in the B-text, suggesting not only that these scenes were in existence by the late 1590s, but that Faustus was associated as much with comic mischief as with damnable magic. In the same play Pistol jocularly refers to Slender as 'Mephistopheles,' again referencing *Doctor Faustus* in a comic context.

Though Marlowe continued to be popular in the early seventeenth century, he did not maintain much status in the English literary world after the Restoration. In 1675, Edward Phillips, in a survey of English poets, referred to him as 'a kind of second Shakespeare ... though inferior both in fame, and merit.' Phillips noted that 'Of all that he hath written to the stage his "Dr. Faustus" hath made the greatest noise with its devils, and such like tragical sport' (*Teatrum Poetarum Anglicorum*, 113–14). Essentially repeating this account in 1687, William Winstanley changed the play's genre, referring to the 'comedy of *Doctor Faustus* with his devils and such like tragical sport, which much pleased the humours of the vulgar' (*Lives of the Most Famous English Poets*, 301). A similarly contemptuous attitude toward Elizabethan theatre is found in Thomas Warton's 1781 *History of English Poetry*, which decries the play as:

> a proof of the credulous ignorance which still prevailed, and a specimen of the subjects which were then not thought improper for tragedy. A tale which at the close of the sixteenth century had the possession of the public theatres of our metropolis, now only frightens the children at a puppet-show in a country-town. (1824 edition, 265)

The play's reduction to childish spectacle in the theatre was matched by its declining reputation in the study.

The Romantic movement of the nineteenth century resurrected *Doctor Faustus*, and critics began to defend Marlowe somewhat from his reputation as an atheistic victim of divine judgment. Charles

Lamb, while observing that Faustus and Barabas (the hero of *The Jew of Malta*) are 'offsprings of a mind which at least delighted to dally with interdicted subjects,' pointed out that 'the holiest minds have sometimes not thought it blameable to counterfeit impiety in the person of another, to bring Vice upon the stage speaking her own dialect'; Lamb compared Marlowe to Milton in this regard (*Specimens of English Dramatic Poets*, 1808; London: Henry G. Bohn, 1854). William Hazlitt also defended Marlowe, writing:

> I cannot find, in Marlowe's play, any proofs of the atheism or impiety attributed to him, unless the beliefs in witchcraft and the Devil can be regarded as such; and at the time he wrote, not to have believed in both, would have been construed into the rankest atheism and irreligion.

He finds Faustus 'a rude sketch, but a gigantic one,' and considers the play Marlowe's greatest work: 'As the outline of the character is grand and daring, the execution is abrupt and fearful. The thoughts are vast and irregular; and the style halts and staggers under them.' Hazlitt does disparage the comic scenes as 'mean and groveling to the last degree' (*Lectures on the Dramatic Literature of the Age of Elizabeth*, 57–8, 64). George Henry Lewes, partial to Goethe's more elevated treatment of the story, found fault with the 'vulgar conception' of Marlowe's *Faustus*; but like Hazlitt he blamed the tastes of Elizabethan audiences. 'The story of Faustus suggests many modes of philosophical treatment, but Marlowe has not availed himself of any: he has taken the popular view of the legend, and given his hero the vulgarest motives.' He excuses Marlowe by saying that 'another and higher mode of treatment might have been less acceptable to the audience ... Had it been metaphysical, they would not have understood it,' though he allows himself to wonder wistfully, 'What would not Shakespeare have made of it?' (*Life and Works of Goethe*, Vol. II, 284).

By the late nineteenth century this somewhat condescending attitude toward Marlowe and *Faustus* began to dissipate. *Fin-de-siècle* freethinkers such as J. A. Symonds championed Marlowe as a heroic rebel, the poet of 'man's ever-craving thirst for beauty, power, knowledge,' in revolt 'against the given order of the world' (*Marlowe: The Critical Heritage*, 135). Algernon Charles Swinburne not only romanticized Marlowe in his poetry ('With mouth of gold, and morning in his eyes'), but defended him in criticism from earlier dismissals (*Tristram of Lyonesse*, l. 102). Of *Faustus* he wrote that 'few masterpieces of any age in any language can stand beside this tragic poem …. For the qualities of terror and splendour, for intensity of purpose and sublimity of note' (*The Age of Shakespeare*, 4). Faustus himself became, for some, a figure of humanistic striving, throwing off the imprisoning beliefs of the medieval world. The philosopher George Santayana, in his 1910 essay *Three Philosophical Poets*, lauded Faustus 'for his love of life, for his trust in nature, for his enthusiasm for beauty,' and concluded that 'Marlowe's Faustus is a martyr to everything the Renaissance prized, – power, curious knowledge, enterprise, wealth, and beauty' (Santayana, George, *Three Philosophical Poets* (Cambridge, MA: Harvard UP, 1944).

Transgression and orthodoxy

This question of whether *Doctor Faustus* represented Renaissance Humanist aspiration – in keeping with Marlowe's supposedly transgressive beliefs – or an orthodox depiction of sin and punishment, became a central one in twentieth-century Marlowe criticism. For several critics the play represented a conflict within Marlowe himself. In 1927, Una Ellis-Fermor saw *Doctor Faustus* as a philosophical battleground for Marlowe's own unresolved conflicts with the beliefs of his age:

> The protagonists are man and the spiritual powers that surround him, the scene is set in no spot upon the physical earth, but in the limitless regions of the mind, and the battle is fought, not for kingdoms or crowns, but upon the question of man's ultimate fate. (*Christopher Marlowe*, 87)

Paul Kocher similarly felt, in 1946, that 'the drama is not primarily one of external action but of spiritual conflict within the soul of one man,' noting that 'this theme allows Marlowe congenial opportunities of blaspheming without fear of being called to account' (*Christopher Marlowe*, 104). For Kocher, the play's power derived from the fact that:

> however scornfully Marlowe rejected the system intellectually, it still had a powerful hold of some sort on his imagination and emotions … However desperate his desire to be free, he was bound to Christianity by the surest of chains – hatred mingled with reluctant longing, and fascination much akin to fear. (pp. 118–19)

In an influential 1952 study entitled *The Overreacher*, Harry Levin saw Faustus, along with Marlowe's other heroes and Marlowe himself, as a figure challenging the limits placed on humanist aspiration. Referring to Marlowe's reputation for Epicurianism, Machiavellianism, and atheism, Levin wrote, 'The unholy trinity of Marlowe's heresies, violating the taboos of medieval orthodoxy, was an affirmation of the strongest drives that animated the Renaissance and have shaped our modern outlook' (p. 26). Levin saw Marlowe identifying not only with Faustus but with Mephistopheles, 'who suffers with Faustus like a second self yet also plays the cosmic ironist, wise in his guilty knowledge and powerful in his defeated rebellion'. Also in 1952, Nicholas Brooke defined *Doctor Faustus* as 'an inverted morality' in which the hero is unfairly punished for his attempts to challenge human limitations. Brooke noted that 'all the positive statements of the play, supported by the finest verse, are against the declared Christian moral' ('The Moral Tragedy of *Dr. Faustus*', 668). He concluded that 'Marlowe chose deliberately to use the Morality form and to use it perversely, to invert or at least to satirize its normal intention' (p. 669). Brooke compares Marlowe to Blake in his 'bitter and farcical irony' and 'magnificent protest' against a 'cruel God' (p. 686).

A range of other mid-century critics argued for a more orthodox understanding of the play as in keeping with early modern beliefs. J. B. Steane (1964) felt that Brooke and other critics advancing what he called the 'Diabolonian Interpretation' of *Doctor Faustus* 'seem to me to be indulging a wish and presenting the play that probably most readers would *like* Marlowe to have written.' While acknowledging that 'The state of mind which the play expresses is not a simple thing,' Steane asserted that 'on balance it is weighted to accept Faustus as sinful and his fate as inevitable' (*Christopher Marlowe: A Critical Study*, 366). Michael Poirier (1951) similarly argued that Faustus is not a 'martyr of free-thought,' describing him as an Icarus rather than a Prometheus. 'Notwithstanding his intellectual eagerness, Marlowe has not been able to keep up to the end Faustus's rebellion against God,' Poirier argued, noting that to do so would have been an impossibility in Elizabethan England (*Christopher Marlowe*, 143). Poirier asserts that 'paradoxically [Marlowe] achieves a result directly opposite to the one he aims at elsewhere: he strengthens the faith of his Christian audience' (p. 144). Leo Kirschbaum was even more forceful in his 1946 reading, asserting that '*Doctor Faustus* is wholly conventional in its Christian values and is in no sense iconoclastic' ('The Good and Bad Quartos of *Doctor Faustus*', 101). For Kirschbaum, the play's theology was 'rigid' and unambiguous: 'If the modern mind ... sees Marlowe's main character as the noble victim of a tyrannical Deity, it is simply being blind' (p. 102). Such views provided a useful corrective to Promethean readings, and opened the way for more complex explorations of *Doctor Faustus* in relation to its historical and religious context.

Questions about Calvinist theology, predestination, and free will became central to many readings of the text. Is Faustus's failure to repent merely an expression of his inevitable damnation? Max Bluestone, surveying critical thought at the end of the 1960s, found scholars about evenly divided on the question of Faustus's free will, and declared the play to be ambiguous on this point. Pauline Honderich felt that the contradictions resulted from two opposing views of God: 'Marlowe calls up and sets against each other the images both of the benevolent God of the Catholic dispensation and of the harsh and revengeful God of Calvinist doctrine'; only in the end does the Calvinist God win out ('John Calvin and Doctor Faustus,' 12). Martha Tuck Rozett, in *The Doctrine of Election and the Emergence of Elizabethan Tragedy* (1984), argued that while Faustus is predestined to damnation, audiences might nonetheless have expected him to repent, resulting in an intense emotional involvement in the outcome. Rozett contended that *Doctor Faustus* drew its tragic power from the very anxieties aroused by the doctrine of predestination:

> For Elizabethans, the haunting fear that they were living a life predetermined to end in damnation ... made Faustus' life a tragic reflection of what their own could be. Repentance, before Calvin, had been the easy remedy for despair; by the 1580s and 1590s, it could be presented as the unattainable tragic ideal. (pp. 209–10)

Faustus's fate demonstrates 'the central paradox of Puritanism, which declares him morally and intellectually responsible for his own fall' despite his predestined damnation. (p. 240). G. M. Pinciss argued in 1993 that in exploring this problem, Marlowe was dramatizing debates he would have encountered at Cambridge, where the influential Calvinist theologian William Perkins took a hard line on predestination. According to Pinciss, Marlowe's play is:

the product of a number of forces – the controversy between Calvinists and anti-Calvinists that must have impressed him deeply during his years at Cambridge, the expanding power of state censorship, and, surely not to be underestimated, his own personal, poetic, and artistic instincts'. ('Marlowe's Cambridge Years and the Writing of *Doctor Faustus*', 260)

The ideologically minded critics of the 1980s and 1990s felt that in engaging with the play's theological problems, Marlowe implicitly critiqued the belief system that doomed Faustus. Stephen Greenblatt, in his landmark new historicist book *Renaissance Self-Fashioning* (1980), felt that Marlowe's heroes represented subversive, disruptive forces that were nevertheless always contained within the powerful cultural structures of Elizabethan England. 'Marlowe's protagonists rebel against orthodoxy, but they do not do so just as they please,' according to Greenblatt; 'their acts of negation not only conjure up the order they would destroy but seem at times to be themselves conjured up by that very order.' In the case of Faustus, his 'whole career binds him ever more closely to that Christian conception of the body and the mind, that divinity, he thought he was decisively rejecting' (p. 210). In a typical new historicist formulation, Faustus's rebellion is not only contained within the power of Christian orthodoxy, it is created by, and helps to create, that power. Faustus's ironic appropriation of Christ's '*Consummatum est*' is 'limited to the status of brilliant parody,' in Greenblatt's words: 'His blasphemy is the uncanny expression of a perverse, despairing faith' (p. 214).

Jonathan Dollimore, in 1984's *Radical Tragedy*, saw the play as more successfully subversive, an 'interrogative text' that exposed the analogous injustices of religious and political power structures. For practicing 'more than heavenly power permits,' Faustus 'has revealed the limiting structure of Faustus's universe for what it is, heavenly *power*,' and consequently he must be destroyed. However, 'the punitive intervention which validates divine power also compromises it' (p. 118). Alan Sinfield (in *Faultlines*, 1992) also contended that the play enables a critique of Reformation beliefs. Because 'the theological implications of *Faustus* are radically and provocatively indeterminate' (p. 234), there exists 'the possibility, which would also fit the sense most readers have of Marlowe as an author, that at some stage at least the play was written to embarrass protestant doctrine' (p. 235). The fact that the play never resolves the contradictions between 'predestinarian and free-will readings' allows them to 'obstruct, entangle, and choke each other,' while the play's final moments elicit audience sympathy for the doomed Faustus (p. 236). 'If this is what happened, for some at least, then there are two traps in the play. One is set by God for Dr. Faustus; the other is set by Marlowe, for God' (p. 237).

Sinfield recognizes that interpretation of the play's theology is partially dependent on the text one chooses to examine; he finds that many of the B-text passages 'enhance the impression that the Reformation god is at work', though others present 'a more genial alternative' (p. 235). The questions about the relative authority of the A- and B-texts of the play have always been central in the editorial history of *Doctor Faustus*, but recent criticism has also highlighted their theological and ideological importance.

Textual and editorial history

From the time Marlowe's plays began to appear in the nineteenth century, editors recognized the textual problem of the differing 1604 and 1616 versions. The earliest editions, beginning with C. W. Dilke in 1814, favored the longer and later B-text. Alexander Dyce printed both texts in his 1850 edition of Marlowe's works, but argued that the B-text reflected later additions by other hands, and therefore the A-text was more authentic. Other editors, including A. H. Bullen in 1885 and C. F. Tucker Brooke in 1910, followed Dyce in favoring A, but the pendulum then swung the other way, with Frederick Boas's influential 1932 edition using B as the main text (while including alternative scenes from A). Many twentieth-century scholars, led by Leo Kirschbaum in 1946, came to believe the A-text was a 'bad quarto' or memorial reconstruction of the play, and that B, even if it included material by other playwrights, contained more of Marlowe's work. W. W. Greg was of this view, but nonetheless printed both texts side by side in his landmark edition of 1950. Other editors such as Roma Gill (1965) and John Jump (1976) brought out conflated texts that primarily used the longer B-text but included readings from A when those seemed preferable. In an important 1981 article on the play, Michael Warren challenged the idea that either text was preferable: 'both texts have their obscurities and their problems and their misprints, and both are probably faulty in relation to any authorial original, but of that authorial original we can know nothing' ('*Doctor Faustus*: The Old Man and the Text', 153).

More recent editors, including Ormerod and Wortham (1985) and Keefer (1991), have gone back to the A-text, following a widespread rejection of the memorial reconstruction hypothesis and a tendency to reprint the earliest texts accurately rather than trying to reconstruct a hypothetical 'authentic' text. Roma Gill, re-editing the play for the Oxford *Complete Works* in 1990, switched to the A-text. Several critics have pointed out the different ideological implications of the competing versions, though not always with the same conclusions. Keefer, in the introduction to his A version, notes its 'foregrounding of the harshness of Calvinist theology,' which is tempered in B. For Keefer, in the B-text:

> the view that Faustus has the capacity to repent, and is therefore wholly responsible for his sinful failure to do so, supplants the A-text's insistent suggestion that his despairing inability to will his own salvation is due to the withholding of divine grace. (*Doctor Faustus: A 1604 Edition*, lxiv)

Leah Marcus, while allowing that 'the spirituality of A appears more strenuous and psychologically demanding throughout,' argues that its final view of Faustus's fate is less definitive (*Unediting the Renaissance*, 51). She sees the A-Faustus's conflict as internal, allowing at least the possibility of final redemption, whereas the B-text's emphasis on the physical representation of devils and hell, and the fragmentation of Faustus's body, make his damnation more straightforward and unequivocal.

Marcus's argument appeared in her influential 1996 book *Unediting the Renaissance*, which presented *Doctor Faustus* as a test case of 'the relativity of editorial judgment, the ease with which we construct an "original" that will satisfy our own tastes and assumptions' (p. 43). Marcus identified a generational difference between older B-text critics who preferred its 'smoothness, polish,' and use of 'spectacle and special effects to communicate widely acceptable cultural ideals,' and a post-Vietnam group of A-text critics who prefer 'theatrical starkness, iconoclasm, dissonance' (p. 44). This kind of critical self-consciousness, together with questions about the possibility of reconstructing a lost 'original,' has made scholars more hesitant about declaring in favor of one text or the other. Indeed, the existence of both texts keeps alive what Marcus terms 'the "Marlowe effect",' balancing the play 'on the nervous razor edge between transcendent heroism and dangerous blasphemy' (p. 42). The recent tendency has been to consider both texts as independent entities, as in the Bevington/Rasmussen Revels editions of 1993 and 2013 and the David Scott Kastan Norton Critical Edition of 2005. Broadview Press has recently brought out a new edition of the B-text (Mathew R. Martin, 2013) to pair with their 2007 revised edition of Keefer's A-text.

Doctor Faustus and theatrical tradition

A number of important twentieth-century studies explored *Doctor Faustus* in relation to the dramaturgical traditions it inherits and exploits, particularly the medieval and Tudor morality play. In '*Doctor Faustus*: A Case of Conscience', Lily B. Campbell compared Marlowe's play to a Reformation morality drama, Nicholas Woodes's *The Conflict of Conscience*, noting their similar focus on the sin of despair. David Bevington's pioneering 1962 study *From 'Mankind' to Marlowe* called *Doctor Faustus* 'the crowning achievement of Psychomachia drama,' referring to the corpus of plays built around the competition between good and evil forces for the soul of the protagonist (p. 245). In this tradition, Bevington found the source for such characters as the Good and Evil Angels and the play's structure of alternating comic and serious scenes. Bevington saw Marlowe's play as reaching the end of that tradition, centering the familiar moral pattern on a figure of tragic dimensions; Faustus represents a paradoxical break-through 'in its moving tragedy of noble character and its explicit denunciation of moral failure, in its hero's sympathetic aspiration and deplorable degeneracy' (p. 262).

In the same year, Douglas Cole, in *Suffering and Evil in the Plays of Christopher Marlowe*, also traced *Faustus* to its morality roots and defined the ways it transcended them. On the one hand, Marlowe used old-fashioned devices like the angels and the Seven Deadly Sins; on the other, he eschewed the traditional comic Vice in favor of a Mephistopheles who 'has a seriousness and intensity which is unparalleled in any previous theatrical representation of the diabolic' (p. 240). Mephistopheles does not try to deceive Faustus like a morality-play devil, but rather tells him the truth about hell to magnify his own willful self-deceit. In Marlowe's play, 'the moral forces and principles that were once abstracted from man's nature and presented separately as external agents are now within his own being. The battle between good and evil is fought in Faustus' own mind' (p. 242).

Susan Snyder, in 'Marlowe's *Doctor Faustus* as an Inverted Saint's Life' (1966), recognized the interplay of morality play and tragedy in *Faustus*, but added a third pattern based on a parodic inversion of the tradition of hagiography. Faustus's blasphemous rituals, 'miraculous' pranks, and inversions of Scripture all parody elements in traditional accounts of saints. 'The travestied saint's life in *Doctor Faustus* intensifies its tragic effect', according to Snyder, 'increasing the stature of the hero while ensuring his downfall' (p. 577).

Robert Weimann, in *Shakespeare and the Popular Tradition in the Theatre* (1978), emphasized the way Marlowe's Renaissance Humanism transformed the theatrical and homiletic materials from which he constructed *Doctor Faustus*. 'Faustus's aspirations are not inspired by the whisperings of a Vice; they are desires born of a superadded consciousness aimed at "the end of every art"' (p. 184). Weimann saw Marlowe as creating a new kind of character, not only object but subject of dramatic and spiritual conflict:

> This dramatic conflation of corrupter and corrupted cannot be understood solely from a Christian homiletic perspective or solely in terms of a popular theatrical background, but only through an appreciation of the remarkable interaction of both points of view as assimilated within a modern and more practical kind of humanism. (pp. 184–5)

For Weimann, as for other theatrically oriented critics, Marlowe transformed the materials of medieval drama into the new form of Renaissance tragedy.

Biography

Questions about Marlowe's religious beliefs and personal opinions, and their relation to the theology of *Doctor Faustus*, have always been a feature of biographies of Marlowe. F. S. Boas's *Christopher Marlowe, a Biographical and Critical Study* (1940), built on recent discoveries to provide the fullest account then available of Marlowe's death; it also related Faustus's academic dissatisfaction to Marlowe's studies at Cambridge. John Bakeless's *The Tragicall History of Christopher Marlowe* (1942) was another detailed early life, occupying two volumes. Though now in some ways dated, it still provides a wealth of information, including many details about the early performance history of *Faustus*. William Urry's *Christopher Marlowe and Canterbury* (1988) provided information on Marlowe's birthplace, family, upbringing, and early influences. One of the most popular and influential books on Marlowe's life was Charles Nicholl's *The Reckoning* (1992), a gripping though speculative account of Marlowe's death and his relations to the Elizabethan secret service. It shed little light on *Doctor Faustus*, apart from asserting that the central character is inspired in part by Giordano Bruno. Constance Brown Kuriyama, in *Christopher Marlowe: A Renaissance Life* (2002) strove to avoid either the sensationalism or documentary ponderousness she saw in earlier biographies. Her account gives a sense of Marlowe's ordinary daily activity in his periods in Canterbury, Cambridge, and London; it collects the important documents of Marlowe's life in a final appendix. David Riggs's *The World of Christopher Marlowe* (2004) reads Marlowe's life and works together in relation to the political and social world of early modern London. Riggs includes a long chapter on the Faust myth and Marlowe's appropriation of it in terms of his own life. 'In writing *Dr Faustus*, Marlowe projected his predicament onto his protagonist,' Riggs concludes. 'The play registers his awareness that the Church produces sin and damnation for its own ends.... *Dr Faustus* demystifies the Calvinist theology that would and did condemn Christopher Marlowe to destruction and hellfire.' (p. 249). The most recent major biography, Park Honan's 2005 *Christopher Marlowe: Poet and Spy*, focuses on Marlowe's government service. Its reading of *Faustus* focuses on the academic world of Cambridge and Marlowe's familiarity with the hermetic traditions of occult philosophy. The ongoing fascination with Marlowe's life continues to provide new lenses with which to view his most famous play.

Postmodern perspectives

The array of new critical perspectives that emerged in the late twentieth century under the general heading of postmodernism have been productive with regard to Marlowe's *Doctor Faustus*. Some recent

scholarship continues to converge around well-established topics
such as the relationship of the two texts or the interpretation of the
hero with regard to Christian orthodoxy. Kristen Poole, for instance,
in 'Doctor Faustus and Reformation Theology' (2006), challenges
the view that the play has a single theological perspective, arguing
that the coexistence of elements of residual Catholic and Calvinist
belief leave Faustus's situation ambiguous and contradictory. The
traditional critical conflict between orthodox and heterodox views
is based on a fallacious reading of Reformation belief as unitary. As
Poole argues, 'Marlowe and his Doctor Faustus were not alone in
their conflicted relationships to free will, predestination, and, ulti-
mately, God – they shared these feelings of conflict and frustration
with many in the audience' (p. 106).

Other recent studies have begun to view the play in relation to such
topics as gender and sexuality, psychoanalysis, and politics. Marlowe's
sexuality has occasioned much critical discussion. His alleged statement
that 'all they that love not tobacco and boys are fools,' his overt portrayal
of an intense male relationship in *Edward II*, and the homoeroticism of
some of his allusions and images have made his work a focus for critical
work on homosexuality. While many scholars accept Alan Bray's formulation, in *Renaissance Homosexuality* (1982), that a homosexual identity
as such was not possible in Elizabethan England, Marlowe's life and work
clearly foreground homoerotic desire. Queer readings of Marlowe, such
as Jonathan Goldberg's 1992 *Sodometries*, understandably tend to focus
on the more obvious homoerotic content of *Edward II*, but *Faustus* has
made itself accessible to readings that incorporate queer theory. Such
readings can be both challenging and productive. In *Sexuality and Form,
Caravaggio, Marlowe, and Bacon* (2000), Graham Hammill employs Eve
Kosofsky Sedgwick's notion of male homosocial desire to characterize
the relationship between Faustus and Mephistopheles. Hammill writes:

> In *Doctor Faustus* sodomy emerges not as the name for certain acts abhor-
> rent to a homosocial culture, but out of the insight, however dim, that
> homosocial gender roles are being performed, as a kind of mediator
> between the naturalization of theatricality and the infelicities to which all
> performatives are of necessity open. (p. 119)

Hammill illuminates such moments as Mephistopheles's presentation to Faustus of the devil-bride and the spirit Helen, both, of course,

male actors representing commodified females exchanged between men. Hammill's essay also explores the connection between sexuality and the literary in *Doctor Faustus*, focusing on references to the Actaeon myth.

Readings of sexuality in *Doctor Faustus* are often built on twentieth-century traditions of psychoanalysis. Constance Brown Kuriyama understands all of Marlowe's work in terms of psychological notions of identity formation, particularly in relation to parental authority and sexuality. In *Hammer and Anvil* (1980), Kuriyama reads *Doctor Faustus* as an expression of Marlowe's own self-ambivalence, 'a product of complex and conflicting attitudes and feelings, at once sympathetic and hostile to a protagonist who is and is not, but mainly is, Marlowe, whose course of action Marlowe simultaneously approves and condemns' (p. 135). Faustus's rebellion against God is a rebellion of the son against the father, even as his relationship to the demonic is one of sexual submission. Kay Stockholder examines similar themes with respect to Faustus's relation to women in her essay 'Within the Massy Entrailes of the Earth' (1988). For Stockholder, Faustus associates women with sexuality and forbidden magic, the antithesis to a threatening paternal God: 'submission to God represents a filial abasement to a paternal authority that equates sexuality of any kind with forbidden knowledge, civic destruction, and eternal torment' (p. 216). In the end, Stockholder sees Faustus choosing hell and sexuality over this threatening Oedipal father. Another important study that combines psychoanalytic insights with the philosophical approach of phenomenology is Edward A. Snow's 'Marlowe's *Doctor Faustus* and the Ends of Desire' (1977). With special focus on Faustus's soliloquies, Snow reads the character's inner life in terms of the emptiness at the core of Faustus's insatiable desires, connecting this to the themes of gluttony and dismemberment, and what he terms the 'oral-narcissistic dilemma' (p. 89).

Though it has few female characters and rarely deals directly with questions of gender, *Doctor Faustus* has occasioned productive work from feminist scholars. Sara Munson Deats comments that 'From a poststructuralist's perspective, with its focus on gaps and omissions, this virtual absence of women characters looms as particularly significant' (*Sex, Gender and Desire in the Plays of Christopher Marlowe*, 203). In her reading, the play centers on a rejection of the feminine, not only of female characters, but of qualities and values traditionally so gendered. The final scene is for Deats a kind of gender apocalypse, when all traces of the feminine have been expunged:

> ... the banishment of these figures signals the erasure from the world of all traces of a benevolent, merciful providence, and the disappearance of Christ's blood from the firmament – the saving feminine fluid that protects vulnerable humanity from the stern Law of the Name-of-the-Father – and its replacement by the ireful visage of a just and wrathful Deity emblematizes the reinscription of authoritarian patriarchal values that the play dramatizes. (p. 224)

Alison Findlay (1999) undertakes a slightly more hopeful feminist reading of the play by considering what it might have offered to female audiences in the period. On the one hand the few female characters are literally or figuratively demonized as descendants or avatars of Eve. On the other hand, 'the play also allows female spectators to see their own situations represented in the protagonist.' As one who contends with a patriarchal authority that would deny him access to knowledge, Faustus has much in common with early modern women, according to Findlay. Moreover, Mephistopheles is also 'a feminized figure,' defined by lack, deprived of access to heavenly blessings, and reduced to servility to Faustus, 'to be in his chamber or house invisible' like the wife in an early modern conduct book (pp. 383–4). Findlay rereads the play in light of Renaissance women's writings like Amelia Lanyer's defense of female learning, which reframes Eve as a positive intellectual figure. 'In *Doctor Faustus* Marlowe re-presents Eve's tragedy; from a male perspective, it is true, but one in which female spectators could see themselves,' Findlay writes. 'Faustus' growth and self-determination, cut off so brutally, offers an image of the way in which their potential for development is repressed and their power is demonized by a society which took its ultimate authority from patriarchal interpretations of the Bible' (pp. 387–8).

Other contemporary readings view the play from such political perspectives as Marxism and postcolonialism. Simon Shepherd's *Marlowe and the Politics of Elizabethan Theatre* (1986) reads all of Marlowe's plays in terms of relations of power, including those implicit in the theatre itself. His account of *Doctor Faustus* focuses on the way pleasurable spectacle can forestall ideological critique: a process the play sometimes reveals, sometimes embodies. When

Faustus is distracted from his doubts by flattering devils, the scene 'privileges the audience to see the connection between theatrical delight and relations of power' (p. 100). At the end of the play, the audience watches with a kind of double perspective, both empathetic and distanced, 'an eminently privileged sharing of the main character's inner life but simultaneously an awareness of watching a show' (p. 108). Whereas the more psychologically realistic and immersive plays of Shakespeare can lull the audience into a critical sleep, '*Faustus* seems to show specifically what is endemic to Elizabethan theatrical practice, where the very theatricality of presentation offers a knowledge not just about the person represented but about the conditions of viewing that person' (p. 109). Another study that combines an interest in theatrical practice with Marxian scholarship is Richard Halpern's 'Marlowe's Theatre of Night: *Doctor Faustus* and Capital,' from 2004. Halpern sees a parallel between the Mephistopheles/Faustus relationship and the Henslowe/Marlowe relationship, between 'the power relations ... within the fiction of the play and within the reality of the playhouse' (p. 465).

In the 1998 essay 'Service and Slavery in *Doctor Faustus*,' Judith Weil plays on connections between demonic possession and domestic servitude to interrogate the early modern economy that tolerated chattel slavery. Examining the Faustus/Mephistopheles relation as well as the situations of such servants as Robin and Wagner, Weil detects in Marlowe an exposure of some of the contradictions of Elizabethan servitude. Weil writes that 'by historicizing the effects of possession on work and by looking carefully at specific interactions of servants and spirits, we can see that the hows and whys of agency are central questions for Marlowe' (p. 145). For Weil, Marlowe's synthesis of demonic and economic 'possession' implies a political critique. 'Long before the Enlightenment critique of slavery as a violation of individual rights, Renaissance dramatists like Marlowe were stigmatizing a condition widely accepted in their world' (p. 151). Emily Bartels undertakes similar readings of Marlowe's plays in terms of economic and political relations in *Spectacles of Strangeness: Imperialism, Alienation and Marlowe* (1993). Focusing on the 'Otherness' of Marlowe's heroes, Bartels reads the plays in terms of the Elizabethan fascination with alien worlds and peoples, linking it (as Greenblatt had also done) to European imperialism. Tamburlaine and Barabas are more central to her project than Faustus, but in a section entitled 'The Alien at Home,' she addresses how 'Marlowe disrupts the great divide instituted most prominently within imperialist discourse, between Europe as the locus of the self and elsewhere as the locus of the other' (p. 114). In *Doctor Faustus* the European subject *is* the other, Faustus the notorious conjurer; and further, he is subject to the imperialist predation of Lucifer, who wants his soul to 'enlarge his kingdom.' Toni Francis takes these arguments even further in 'Imperialism as Devilry: A Postcolonial Reading of *Doctor Faustus*,' from 2010:

> In attempting to ascertain the place of magic and necromancy in *Doctor Faustus*, I question whether this play was ever meant to probe the actual practice of dark magic, or whether necromancy – and more specifically, selling one's soul to the devil – can be interpreted as a metaphor for a more contemporary form of soul-selling – that is, England's violent and gluttonous domination of the indigenous peoples of Africa, India and the New World represented in the play as England's descent into Hades. (pp. 118–19)

While an extreme reading, Francis's argument reveals the extent to which the language of power, whether voiced by Faustus, Valdes, Mephistopheles, or Lucifer, often echoes the language of imperial conquest.

Criticism of Marlowe and *Faustus* is flourishing in the first decades of the twenty-first century. *Marlowe Studies* has been an annual publication since 2011, and the Marlowe Society of America holds regular conferences. In Robert Logan's 2010 survey of the state of scholarship pertaining to *Doctor Faustus*, he lists more than 30 books and some 80 individual essays published since 2000. His survey and the book that contains it, Sara Munson Deats's *Doctor Faustus: A Critical Guide*, are valuable indices to the state of contemporary studies of the play. Deats and Logan's 2015 publication *Christopher Marlowe at 450* contains another assessment of *Faustus* criticism. *The Cambridge Companion to Christopher Marlowe* (ed. Patrick Cheney, 2004) and *Christopher Marlowe in Context* (edited by Emily C. Bartels and Emma Smith, 2013) also provide good overviews of the critical field, with a number of chapters in each volume dealing with *Doctor Faustus*. Marlowe's powerful and perplexing play is evidently far from exhausting its power to provoke.

Further Reading

Editions of the play

Barnet, Sylvan, ed., *Christopher Marlowe: Doctor Faustus* (New York: New American Library, 1969). Signet Classics edition, based on the B-text, with accompanying critical essays and excerpts from *The English Faust Book*.

Bevington, David and Eric Rasmussen, eds, *Doctor Faustus, A- and B-Texts (1604, 1616), The Revels Plays* (Manchester: Manchester University Press, 1993). Important critical edition of both texts, on which the Revels Student Edition, used for this volume, is based. Includes extensive introduction and discussion of textual issues, including the reordering of the clown scenes.

Bevington, David and Eric Rasmussen, eds, *Doctor Faustus, The A- and B-Texts (1604, 1616): A Parallel-Text Edition* (Manchester: Manchester University Press, 2013). The Revels Student Edition on which this handbook is based shows the two texts on facing pages for easy comparison.

Greg, W. W., *Marlowe's Doctor Faustus, 1604–1616: Parallel Texts* (Oxford: Clarendon Press, 1950). Landmark parallel text edition in original spelling. Argues for the superiority of the B-text.

Kastan, David Scott, ed., *Christopher Marlowe: Doctor Faustus* (New York: Norton, 2005). Norton Critical Edition containing both the A- and B-texts in modern spelling, along with contextual materials and a valuable collection of essays from throughout the history of *Faustus* criticism.

Keefer, Michael, ed., *Doctor Faustus: A 1604 Edition* (Peterborough: Broadview Press, 1991, rev. 2007).

Martin, Mathew R., ed., *Doctor Faustus: The B-Text* (Peterborough: Broadview Press, 2013).

Ormerod, David and Christopher Wortham, eds, *Christopher Marlowe: Doctor Faustus, The A-Text* (Nedlands: University of Western Australia Press, 1985).

Collections of criticism

Bartels, Emily C. and Emma Smith, eds, *Christopher Marlowe in Context* (Cambridge: Cambridge University Press, 2013). A collection encompassing Marlowe's works, world, and reception.

Cheney, Patrick, *The Cambridge Companion to Christopher Marlowe* (Cambridge: Cambridge University Press, 2004). Includes an essay by Thomas Healy on *Doctor Faustus*, as well as several more general essays that consider the play in relation to Marlowe's career and context.

Deats, Sarah Munson, ed., *Doctor Faustus: A Critical Guide* (London: Continuum, 2010). A collection of essays on the play, including a performance history and an invaluable guide to recent criticism.

Deats, Sarah Munson and Robert Logan, eds, *Christopher Marlowe at 450* (Farnham, Surrey: Ashgate, 2015). Includes Deats's overview of the critical controversies surrounding *Doctor Faustus*, as well as a series of essays on Marlowe in contemporary contexts.

Leech, Clifford and A. Marlowe, eds, *Collection of Critical Essays* (Twentieth Century Views) (Englewood Cliffs, NJ: Prentice Hall, 1964). Contains contributions by many of the important critics of Marlowe from the first half of the twentieth century, including W. W. Greg's essay on *Faustus*.

MacLure, Millar, *Marlowe: The Critical Heritage, 1588–1896* (London: Routledge, 1979). A digest of the first three centuries of Marlowe criticism.

Oz, Avraham, *Marlowe: New Casebooks* (Basingstoke: Palgrave Macmillan, 2003). An important collection of essays, including several addressing *Doctor Faustus*.

The Elizabethan theatre

Astington, John, *Actors and Acting in Shakespeare's Time: The Art of Stage Playing* (Cambridge: Cambridge University Press, 2010). Includes material on Edward Alleyn and the Admiral's Men.

Eccles, Christine, *The Rose Theatre* (London: Nick Hern Books, 1990). A history and description of the theatre where the first recorded performance of *Doctor Faustus* occurred, including detailed archeological evidence about its rediscovery and excavation.

Foakes, R. A. and R. T. Rickert, eds, *Henslowe's Diary* (Cambridge: Cambridge University Press, 1961, 2nd edition 2002). The most important document in Elizabethan theatre history; contains information on the earliest recorded performances of *Doctor Faustus*.

Foakes, R. A., ed., *The Henslowe Papers* (London: Scolar Press, 1977). Other important documents from the Alleyn/Henslowe collection at Dulwich College, relating to the performances of the Admiral's Men.

Gurr, Andrew, *The Shakespearean Stage*, 4th edition (Cambridge: Cambridge University Press, 2009). Thoroughly revised, reliable guide to early modern theatrical conditions.

Gurr, Andrew, *Shakespeare's Opposites: The Admiral's Company, 1594–1625* (Cambridge: Cambridge University Press, 2012). The first history of the company that performed Marlowe's plays.

Intellectual and cultural context

Agrippa, Cornelius, *Of Occult Philosophy* (1531), trans. J. F. (London: 1651).

Beard, Thomas, *The Theatre of God's Judgments* (London: 1597).

Calvin, John, *The Institutes of the Christian Religion*, trans. Thomas Norton (London: 1561).

Jones, John Henry, ed., *The English Faust Book: A Critical Edition* (Cambridge: Cambridge University Press, 1994). Includes a modern-spelling text marking differences between the German and English versions.

Performance history

Alexander, Nigel, *The Performance of Christopher Marlowe's Dr. Faustus* (Chatterton Lecture on an English Poet) (Oxford: Oxford University Press, 1972).

Flanagan, Hallie, *Arena* (New York: Duell, Sloan and Peace, 1940).

Grotowski, Jerzy, *Towards a Poor Theatre*, ed., Eugenio Barba (London: Methuen, 1968).

Holroyd, Michael, *A Strange Eventful History* (New York: Farrar, Strauss, and Giroux, 2009).

Houseman, John, *Run-through* (New York: Simon and Schuster, 1972).

Junor, Penny, *Burton: The Man Behind the Myth*, (New York: St Martin's, 1985).

Mountford, William, *The Life and Death of Doctor Faustus, Made into a Farce. … With the Humours of Harlequin and Scaramouche, etc.*, (London: 1697).

Rich, John, *An Exact Description of the Two Fam'd Entertainments of Harlequin Doctor Faustus: with the Grand Masque of the Heathen Deities: and the Necromancer, or Harlequin Doctor Faustus* (London: printed for T. Payne, 1724).

Speaight, Robert, *William Poel and the Elizabethan Revival* (London: Heinemann, 1954).

Tydemann, William, *Doctor Faustus: Text and Performance* (Basingstoke: Macmillan, 1984).

Film and video

Aebischer, Pascale, 'Renaissance Tragedy on Film,' in *The Cambridge Companion to English Renaissance Tragedy*, ed. Emma Smith and Garrett A. Sullivan, (Cambridge: Cambridge University Press, 2010): 115–31.

Doctor Faustus, dir. Nevill Coghill and Richard Burton, Sony Pictures Home Entertainment, 1968.

Doctor Faustus, dir. Dominic Dromgoole, Shakespeare's Globe, 2011, Globe Player (https://globeplayer.tv/videos/doctor-faustus).

Faust, dir. Jan Švankmajer, Pandora Cinema, 1994.

Biographies of Marlowe

Bakeless, John, *The Tragicall History of Christopher Marlowe* (Hamden, CT: Archon Books, 1942).

Boas, F. S., *Christopher Marlowe, a Biographical and Critical Study* (Oxford: Clarendon, 1940).

Honan, Park, *Christopher Marlowe: Poet & Spy* (Oxford: Oxford University Press, 2005).

Kuriyama, Constance Brown, *Christopher Marlowe: A Renaissance Life* (Ithaca, NY: Cornell UP, 2002).

Nicholl, Charles, *The Reckoning: The Murder of Christopher Marlowe* (New York: Harcourt Brace, 1992).

Riggs, David, *The World of Christopher Marlowe* (New York: Henry Holt, 2004).

Urry, William, *Christopher Marlowe and Canterbury* (London: Faber, 1988).

Criticism

Bartels, Emily Carroll, *Spectacles of Strangeness: Imperialism, Alienation, and Marlowe* (Philadelphia, PA: University of Pennsylvania, 1993).

Bevington, David M., *From Mankind to Marlowe; Growth of Structure in the Popular Drama of Tudor England* (Cambridge: Harvard University Press, 1962).

Bluestone, Max, 'Libido Speculandi: Doctrine and Dramaturgy in Contemporary Interpretations of Marlowe's *Doctor Faustus*,' in *Reinterpretations of Elizabethan Drama*, ed. Norman Rabkin (New York: Columbia University Press, 1969) 33–88.

Brooke, Nicholas, 'The Moral Tragedy of *Dr. Faustus*,' *Cambridge Journal* 5 (1952): 663–87.

Bruster, Douglas, 'Christopher Marlowe and the Verse/Prose Bilingual System,' *Marlowe Studies: An Annual* 1 (2011): 141–65.

Campbell, Lily B. '*Doctor Faustus*: A Case of Conscience,' *PMLA* 67.2 (1952): 219–39.

Cole, Douglas, *Suffering and Evil in the Plays of Christopher Marlowe* (Princeton, NJ: Princeton University Press, 1962).

Deats, Sara Munson, *Sex, Gender and Desire in the Plays of Christopher Marlowe* (Newark, DE: U of Delaware Press, 1997).

Dollimore, Jonathan, *Radical Tragedy: Religion, Ideology and Power in the Drama of Shakespeare and His Contemporaries* (Chicago: University of Chicago Press, 1984).

Ellis-Fermor, Una, *Christopher Marlowe* (London: Methuen, 1927).

Empson, William, *Faustus and the Censor* (Oxford: Basil Blackwell, 1987).

Findlay, Allison, *A Feminist Perspective on Renaissance Drama* (Oxford: Blackwell, 1999).

Francis, Toni, 'Imperialism as Devilry: A Postcolonial Reading of *Doctor Faustus*,' in *Doctor Faustus: A Critical Guide*, ed. Sara Munson Deats (London: Continuum, 2010) 111–23.

Greenblatt, Stephen, *Renaissance Self-Fashioning: From More to Shakespeare* (Chicago: University of Chicago Press, 1980).

Greg, W. W., 'The Damnation of Faustus,' *Modern Language Review* 41 (1946): 97–107.

Hammill, Graham, *Sexuality and Form, Caravaggio, Marlowe, and Bacon* (Chicago: University of Chicago Press, 2000).

Kirschbaum, Leo, 'The Good and Bad Quartos of *Doctor Faustus*,' *Library* 26 (1946): 272–94.

Kocher, Paul H., *Christopher Marlowe: A Study of His Thought, Learning and Character* (New York: Russell and Russell, 1946).

Kuriyama, Constance Brown, *Hammer or Anvil: Psychological Patterns in Christopher Marlowe's Plays* (New Brunswick, NJ: Rutgers University Press, 1980).

Levin, Harry, *The Overreacher: A Study of Christopher Marlowe* (Cambridge: Harvard UP, 1952).

Marcus, Leah S., *Unediting the Renaissance Shakespeare, Marlowe, Milton* (London: Routledge, 1996).

Pinciss, G. M., 'Marlowe's Cambridge Years and the Writing of *Doctor Faustus*,' *SEL* 33 (1993): 249–64.

Poole, Kristen, 'Dr. Faustus and Reformation Theology,' in *Early Modern English Drama: A Critical Companion*, ed. Garrett A. Sullivan, Jr., Patrick Cheney, and Andrew Hadfield (New York: Oxford University Press, 2006): 96–107.

Poirier, Michael, *Christopher Marlowe* (London: Chatto and Windus, 1951).

Rozett, Martha Tuck, *The Doctrine of Election and the Emergence of Elizabethan Tragedy* (Princeton, NJ: Princeton University Press, 1984).

Shepherd, Simon, *Marlowe and the Politics of Elizabethan Theatre* (New York: St Martin's, 1986).

Sinfield, Alan, *Faultlines: Cultural Materialism and the Politics of Dissident Reading* (Berkeley, CA: University of California Press, 1992).

Snow, Edward A., 'Doctor Faustus and the Ends of Desire,' in *Two Renaissance Mythmakers*, ed. Alvin B. Kernan (Baltimore: Johns Hopkins University Press, 1977) 70–110.

Snyder, Susan, 'Marlowe's Doctor Faustus as an Inverted Saint's Life,' *Studies in Philology* 63 (1966): 565–77.

Steane, J. B., *Christopher Marlowe: A Critical Study* (Cambridge: Cambridge University Press, 1964).

Stockholder, Kay, '"Within the massy entrails of the earth": Faustus's Relation to Women,' in *A Poet and a Filthy Play-Maker: New Essays on Christopher Marlowe*, ed. Kenneth Friedenreich, Roma Gill, and Constance Kuriyama (New York: AMS Press, 1988), 203–19.

Warren, Michael J., 'Doctor Faustus: The Old Man and the Text,' *English Literary Renaissance* 11 (1981): 111–47.

Weil, Judith, '"Full Possession": Service and Slavery in *Doctor Faustus*,' in *Marlowe, History, and Sexuality: New Critical Essays on Christopher Marlowe*, ed. Paul Whitfield White (New York: AMS Press, 1998).

Weimann, Robert, *Shakespeare and the Popular Tradition in the Theatre* (Baltimore: Johns Hopkins University Press, 1978).

Index